Gayle Soucek

Conures

Everything About Purchase, Care, Nutrition, and Behavior

D0911272

BARRON'S

CONTENTS

Introduction to Conures   5

Taxonomy and Etymology   5

The Typical Conure   6

The Conure in Captivity   7

Personality and
Pet Potential   8

Adult Conures vs. Baby
Conures as Pets   9

Common Pet Species   9

Hybrid Conures   11

Choosing Your Conure   13

Selecting a Healthy Bird   13

Where to Find a
Pet Conure   14

Health Guarantees   19

Preparing for the
New Arrival   19

Transporting   19

Finding an Avian
Veterinarian   20

The First Veterinarian
Visit   20

Quarantine   21

The First Days at Home   21

Healthy Happy Housing   23

Types of Cages   23

Cage Shape and Design   23

Cage Sizing   24

Bar Spacing   24

Cage Materials   25

The Zinc Controversy   25

Cage Placement   26

Perches and Other
Cage Accessories   28

Travel Cages   30

Lighting and Air Quality   31

Cleaning the Cage   33

Disinfection   34

**Playtime for
Your Conure**   37

The Importance of Play   37

Choosing Proper Toys   37

Simple Toys   40

Making Bird Toys   40

Foot Toys   41

Play Stands   41

Interactive Games   42

**Understanding
Your Conure**   45

What to Expect
from Your Conure   45

What Your Conure
Expects from You   46

Working with
Your Conure   48

Wing Clipping vs.
Free Flight   48

Height and Dominance   49

Step Up Command   49

Speech Training   50

Trick Training   50

Problem Behaviors   53

Healthy Nutrition   57

Seed Diets   57

Formulated Diets   60

Grains, Beans, and Nuts   61

Fruits and Veggies   61

People Foods   62

Water   63

HOW-TO: Cooking
for Conures   64

**Your Conure in
Health and Disease**   67

Common Diseases   68

Bacterial Infections   68

Fungal Infections   70

Viral Infections   70

HOW-TO: Accidents and
First Aid   74

**Select Conure Species
and Descriptions   77**

Understanding Taxonomy   77

Genus *Aratinga*   78

Genus *Pyrrhura*   85

Other Genera   88

Information   92

Index   94

INTRODUCTION TO CONURES

Not all species are available— some are very rare or difficult to maintain in captivity—but you should have no problem choosing from a wide variety of suitable pets.

The New World that the first European explorers discovered was a place of beauty and variety. From arid deserts through scrubby savannahs and lush tropical forests, the land teemed with birds and animals never before seen. Gaudily colored parrots roamed the skies and screeched from the forest canopies. Early ornithologists attempted to create some order from the chaos, and began to group the birds according to common characteristics. It was thus that the genus *Conurus* was born.

Taxonomy and Etymology

Conurus is Latin, from the Greek *Kon* (cone) + *ouros* (tailed), and was used to classify the dozens of species of long-tailed parakeets that originally ranged from the southeastern United States, throughout Mexico and the Caribbean, and down through Central and South America

all the way to Tierra del Fuego. The original *Conurus* genus only included a small portion of the birds we call conures today, mostly those in the current genus *Aratinga*. Taxonomy is rarely static, and soon the long-tailed parakeets were regrouped and renamed, and genus *Conurus* disappeared from the lexicon. However, the common name "conure" has remained in use in the avicultural, if not the scientific, community.

Today, the term *conure* is not recognized by the American Ornithologists' Union, who simply refer to the various species as parakeets, and there's precious little agreement among aviculturists about which species belong under the conure umbrella. The International Conure Association (ICA) recognizes approximately 57 species and subspecies of *Aratinga* (from a Tupi Indian name for parrot, literally "small macaw") and roughly 36 species and subspecies of *Pyrrhura*, from the Greek *Pyrros* (fire) + *ouro*

The Quaker (or Monk) parakeet (**Myiopsitta monachus**) *is sometimes grouped with conures by taxonomists, but is usually considered a separate breed by aviculturists.*

(tail), which refers to their typically reddish-brown tails. In addition, ICA recognizes seven other mostly single species genera, including *Cyanoliseus, Enicognathus, Guaruba, Nandayus, Leptosittaca, Ognorhynchus,* and the now-extinct *Conuropsis.*

Other sources include the Quaker (or Monk) Parakeet, *Myiopsitta monachus,* and the Thick-billed Parrot, *Rhynchopsitta pachyrhyncha,* along with the various *Brotogeris* and *Bolborhynchus* species into the conure group due to some similarity in characteristics and range. Yet others argue that the Golden (or Queen of Bavaria's) conure, *Guaruba guarouba* is really a macaw and not a conure. As you can see, taxonomy isn't simple or clearly defined! For the purposes of this book, I'll include only the species recognized by ICA, and will focus mostly on common pet species in the *Aratinga, Pyrrhura,* and *Nandayus* genera.

The Typical Conure

In truth, it's difficult to define the "typical" conure. Conures range in size from the tiny but beautiful Painted conure, *Pyrrhura picta,* which weighs in at about 55 grams (1.8 oz.) and 8½ inches (21.5 cm) long, to the attractive Greater Patagonian conure, *Cyanoliseus patagonus bloxami,* which weighs about 390 grams (12.5 oz) and stands 18 inches (46 cm) from head to tail. They live in a wide variety of climates, from scrubby cactus-filled deserts to lush grasslands to cool mountain forests. Some conures are arboreal, spending most of their time in the high treetops, while others are partly terrestrial, foraging for food on the ground. Many nest in hollowed out tree cavities like the majority of other parrot species, but some conures make their nests in active arboreal termite nests. The Patagonian conure burrows in the sides of cliffs, giving it the nickname "burrowing parrot."

One genus, which consisted of the now extinct Carolina parakeet *Conuropsis c. carolinensis* and its subspecies, *Conuropsis c. ludovicianus,* (the Louisiana parakeet, also extinct) was native to the United States, and ranged from the Ohio Valley to the Gulf of Mexico, and from the East coast all the way westward to the Dakotas and eastern Colorado. These birds blanketed the skies in flocks of thousands during the early 1800s, but were hunted heavily by farmers

The beautiful Painted conure is the smallest member of the conure family.

The Conure in Captivity

Tame conures can make wonderful pets. Even skittish wild birds, especially the small but beautiful *Pyrrhuras*, have long been treasured as aviary specimens in Europe. For these reasons, conures are very popular in the pet trade. TRAFFIC International, a wildlife trade monitoring network, reports that during the period from 1982 through 1988, over 1.8 million neotropical parrots—the group that includes conures, macaws, and Amazon parrots—were legally exported for trade, and sadly, perhaps as many as 4 million total were captured but the remainder either died or were illegally exported. In the United States, the Wild Bird Conservation Act of 1992 effectively ended all importation of parrots, which means that all pet conures born after that year have been bred in captivity.

The Maroon-bellied conure has good pet potential.

protecting their crops, and hunters seeking the beautiful feathers for ladies' millinery. However, even these pressures don't seem to be enough to have resulted in such a mass extinction, so scientists suspect that some type of disease outbreak, probably from domestic poultry, contributed to their final demise. The last known wild specimen was shot in Florida in 1904, and the last captive bird, a male named "Incas," died in the Cincinnati Zoo in 1918.

Nanday conures are affectionate but sometimes-noisy clowns.

Luckily, many of the previously imported birds were placed into breeding situations, and because most conures are relatively prolific breeders, there's since been a steady stream of tame hand-fed babies in the pet trade. These birds (at least those from reputable aviculturists) are well socialized and free of most of the parasites and diseases that plagued wild-caught parrots.

Personality and Pet Potential

One thing that does define the typical conure is its personality, which is playful, affectionate, and comical. These natural clowns love to amuse, and will bond strongly to their owners. They are often opinionated and bossy, but with hearts of gold. Some folks feel that the *Pyrrhura* species require frequent handling to remain tame and avoid a tendency toward nippiness, but all conures require a lot of love and attention and should always be a part of your family's daily life.

Most conures love water, and will enjoy splashing around in a shallow crock or being gently misted with a spray bottle. Some even like to shower with their owners, and stick-on suction shower perches are available from bird supply retailers. All conures can learn to talk (although not all will), but their voices are usually not as clear as some other species such as Amazons and African greys. They're active and highly intelligent birds, and easily pick up on simple tricks. They love to snuggle, and enjoy hiding and burrowing under papers or blankets, which can put them at risk of being crushed by an inattentive owner. Many species, especially Nandays, love to roll onto their backs and play with foot toys.

Although conures are nearly perfect in every way, they do come with a downside. They're vocal birds that can easily cross the line into loud and screechy. In general, *Aratinga spp.*, Nandays, and Patagonians are the worst (read: loudest) offenders, and the *Pyrrhura spp.* are often a bit quieter. However, virtually all parrots are noisy, so it comes down to a matter of personal tolerance. If you want to share your life with one of these beautiful birds, know that it will not be a quiet life. If peace and solitude are your goals, a parrot, especially a conure, is not the pet for you. Some individual birds might surprise their owners and turn out to be relatively quiet pets, but typically that is not the parrot's nature. Don't purchase a conure thinking you can change it; that's like expecting a dog not to bark, or a cat not to purr.

Adult Conures vs. Baby Conures as Pets

Tame conures of any age are capable of becoming wonderful pets. It's not true that you must purchase a baby for it to bond to you. The only issue with purchasing an adult conure is that you will be facing whatever emotional baggage the bird is carrying. If the adult bird is coming from a loving and stable home, it will likely be a loving and stable pet. If, on the other hand, it was abused, neglected, or even benignly ignored, it might be angry, depressed, or distrustful of humans. However, I've adopted many birds in the latter category, and they're usually smart enough to equate a new home with a fresh start. Some of the tamest pets I've had have been formerly neglected parrots that are grateful to have a new person to love and play with.

If you purchase a newly weaned baby conure, you're essentially starting with a clean slate. It will be up to you to socialize and guide the chick as it learns its place in your household. There is, however, one point I feel very strongly about: Do not *ever* consider buying a chick that is not yet fully weaned! Hand-feeding a parrot chick is a delicate and time-consuming skill, and one that is fraught with potential dangers. A baby parrot is extremely vulnerable at this time, both physically and emotionally. A few breeders might attempt to convince you that weaning the chick is a bonding process that will

The breathtaking Queen of Bavaria's (or Golden) conure is rare, and should be kept in designated breeding programs.

ensure a tame pet. This is nonsense—the only one that will benefit is the breeder who doesn't have to spend the time rearing the chick through weaning. Most folks wouldn't think of purchasing a puppy that still needed to be bottle-fed, and yet baby parrots are much more fragile and prone to potentially deadly results from improper hand-feeding techniques. Wait until your conure is completely weaned and self-sufficient before you uproot it into a new environment. You'll both be much happier.

Common Pet Species

As mentioned earlier, not all conure species are available as pets. Some species are extremely

rare in their native countries, and captive individuals are housed primarily in zoos or captive breeding programs designed for conservation purposes. Others might not be rare, but didn't demonstrate enough of the traits (either coloring or personality) to help them get established in the pet trade. Either way, there are plenty of beautiful and easily available species to choose from, so a prospective conure owner shouldn't need to look far for a great pet.

Genus *Aratinga*

In general, *Aratinga* conures are usually larger and more colorful than some of the other species, albeit with a few exceptions. (I'll discuss selected species in more detail in Chapter 8, but below is a listing of a few of the more commonly kept pets.) In each case, I'm listing the nominate or main species. Subspecies of each of these might be available as well, although subspecies are often misidentified as the nominate in the pet trade. Unless you are breeding the birds and wish to establish a pure bloodline, the subspecies won't have any effect on your bird's pet quality. I've also included other common names. Many of these species are known by several names in different parts of the world, but below are the most frequently encountered.

✔ Blue-crowned conure, *Aratinga a. acuticaudata*. Also known as Sharp-tailed conure.
✔ Brown-throated conure, *Aratinga p. pertinax*. Also known as St. Thomas conure.
✔ Cactus conure, *Aratinga c. cactorum*.
✔ Cherry-headed conure, *Aratinga erythrogenys*. Also known as Red-masked conure.
✔ Dusky-headed conure, *Aratinga weddellii*.
✔ Finsch's conure, *Aratinga finschi*.
✔ Golden-capped conure, *Aratinga a. auricapilla*.

✔ Jenday conure, *Aratinga jandaya*.
✔ Mitred conure, *Aratinga m. mitrata*.
✔ Orange-fronted conure, *Aratinga c. canicularis*. Also know as Half-moon conure.
✔ Peach-fronted conure, *Aratinga a. aurea*.
✔ Red-fronted conure, *Aratinga w. wagleri*.
✔ Sun conures, *Aratinga solstitialis*.
✔ White-eyed conure, *Aratinga l. leucophthalma*.

Genus *Pyrrhura*

Pyrrhura conures are typically smaller and less flashy than their *Aratinga* cousins, but they are nevertheless beautiful and make sweet pets. They're often quieter than their larger cousins as well, so they can be excellent apartment birds. These small conures pack a big parrot personality into a small package! Below are the most commonly available species.

✔ Black-capped conure, *Pyrrhura r. rupicola*.
✔ Green-cheeked conure, *Pyrrhura m. molinae*.
✔ Maroon-bellied conure, *Pyrrhura f. frontalis*.
✔ Maroon-tailed conure, *Pyrrhura m. melanura*. Also known as Black-tailed or Souance's conure.
✔ Painted conure, *Pyrrhura picta*.

Other Genera

There are a few other genera of conures that are commonly encountered as pets. Most make excellent companions, but the Queen of Bavaria's (also known as Golden) conure is rare in the wild and expensive in captivity. Up until a few years ago, federal permits were required to breed and sell this bird across state lines. The laws protecting it from careless breeding have been dissolved, but the species is no less rare than before, and belongs in cooperative captive breeding and management programs, not in the pet trade.

✔ Queen of Bavaria's conure, *Guaruba guarouba.* Also known as Golden conure. This species is often identified as *Aratinga guarouba,* but most taxonomists now place it in its own genus.
✔ Nanday conure, *Nandayus nenday.*
✔ Austral conure, *Enicognathus f. ferrugineus.*
✔ Slender-billed conure, *Enicognathus leptorhynchus.*
✔ Patagonian conure, *Cyanoliseus p. patagonus.*
✔ Greater Patagonian conure, *Cyanoliseus p. patagonus.*

Hybrid Conures

Hybrids occur when two different species cross-breed. In dogs, hybrids are called by the much less flattering name, mutts. Hybridization can only occur within a genus, or between two closely related genera. For example, a Sun and a Jenday conure could cross-breed, but a Jenday would not be able to produce offspring with an African grey parrot. Hybridization rarely occurs in the wild, but sometimes happens intentionally in aviculture when breeders set out to produce "new" parrot breeds. The problem with this thinking is that many of these species are critically endangered in their native ranges. To dilute valuable genetic material in this manner means that we might not have viable and pure gene pools to turn to if we ever wish to attempt repopulation of wild flocks.

As it is, many subspecies have been lost or muddied through careless breeding. This doesn't in any way impact their pet qualities, but it does bring into question the very survival of the original species as found in nature. I'm certainly not saying that existing hybrids are

Cactus conures are sometimes confused with the more common African Senegal parrot.

inferior to the "pure" species, or any less deserving of love, but I do believe that intentional crossbreeding is poor practice, and one that should not be encouraged. After all, we are the stewards of these beautiful and often rare birds, and it's up to us to ensure their future through careful and responsible management.

CHOOSING YOUR CONURE

Conures are popular pets, and can be found almost anywhere pet birds are sold.

In a perfect world, a potential conure owner would spend a great deal of time researching and preparing before finding the ideal bird. The bird would be healthy, affectionate, well behaved, and would talk up a storm, yet could also play quietly when its owners wanted some peace. Life would be good!

Unfortunately, real life rarely works out that well. Many pet bird owners acquire their pet on a whim, and might be totally unprepared for the level of care and interaction required by these intelligent creatures. The bird might have health and/or behavioral issues, and no good reason to trust humans in general. Either way, the relationship is off to a rocky start.

If you have not yet purchased your conure, this chapter can guide you through some of the pitfalls. If you're holding this book with

Green-cheeked conures are affectionate and readily available pets.

one hand, and holding a strange little feathered alien with the other, then perhaps this chapter can offer some tips on how to proceed.

Selecting a Healthy Bird

The first step is to choose a healthy bird. A sick conure is obviously not going to be a playful and interactive pet; instead it will be focusing its energies on survival. Even a non-life threatening illness will sap the bird's strength and vitality. Please do not purchase a sick conure in order to rescue it! Although it's an admirable intent, few parrot diseases respond to simple and easy home cures. More than likely, you'll be facing substantial veterinary bills, time-consuming treatments, and the very real possibility that the bird might not survive anyway. If you already own other birds, you'll be putting their lives at extreme risk if the disease is communicable (and most are). If you spot a bird for sale that appears ill, inform the seller, then leave immediately. Be certain to shower and change clothes before you visit another bird store or handle your own pets, or you could unwittingly transmit a deadly disease. In fact, I recommend the same precautions after handling any strange birds, because it's possible they are asymptomatic carriers of disease.

Where to Find a Pet Conure

If you're looking for a particular species, you might have to search a little further, but several of the common conure species are readily available in the pet trade.

Pet Stores

Most pet stores carry at least a few birds, especially smaller pets such as canaries, finches, and budgies. That doesn't necessarily mean that the store has a great deal of knowledge or experience with birds. Always begin by looking around and asking questions. Does the store look and smell clean? Are the animals caged appropriately? Are food and water dishes clean and full? Keep in mind that parrots are messy, and often like to toss their food or dunk it in their water dishes, but the staff should be making a reasonable attempt to keep up.

How much do the employees seem to know about the animals in their care? If you need a resource for information after you purchase your conure, do you feel comfortable that the staff can answer your questions, or at least point you in the right direction? Does the store specialize in a certain type of pet? For example, the store you're considering might be the local expert on fish, but only carry a few birds to round out the inventory. On the other hand, if

the shop specializes in birds, it's likely you'll have a wonderful place to turn when you need advice. Finally, do they carry all or most of the supplies you'll need for your pet? If you can find just the right store, you'll benefit from their care and expertise, and they'll benefit from your loyalty and word-of-mouth advertising.

Conure Breeders

Buying directly from a breeder insures you'll be working with someone who has some in-depth experience and familiarity with conures. Unfortunately, like pet stores, there are good breeders and bad breeders. Often, the bad ones don't stay around very long, because their inexperience or lack of proper care prevents their birds from producing chicks. But unlike pet stores, where you can look around and judge the facilities for yourself, it's doubtful that a breeder will allow you to inspect his or her aviary. Breeding birds are sensitive, and allowing strangers in the aviary can have disastrous results. Panicked parent birds can break eggs, desert their nests, or even kill their chicks due to displaced aggression. Strangers can track in deadly diseases, especially if they're making the rounds of other bird facilities. How, then, do you judge the quality and expertise of the aviculturist?

1. You can ask for recommendations from previous clients, or from the veterinarian that services the breeder's birds. Veterinarians might be unwilling to disclose sensitive negative information, but just verifying that a breeder has a working relationship with a qualified vet is a good first step.

2. How well does the breeder answer your questions? Someone who is impatient, vague, or appears lacking in knowledge might not be the person you want to purchase from. After all, the breeder should be there to serve as a resource for your future needs and questions.

3. How does the person handle his or her birds? Chicks raised with confidence and love usually make desirable pets. Chicks that are rarely handled and poorly socialized might never live up to their full pet potential.

4. Do you feel rushed to make a decision or leave a deposit? Caring breeders want their babies to go to loving and permanent homes, so don't be surprised if it seems that the breeders are grilling you to decide if you're worthy of their beloved chicks. If you come across someone in a rush to make a sale, that person does not have the best interests of the bird at heart.

In the end, you'll be best served by following your instincts. Never purchase a conure on a whim. Buying a parrot is a long-term commitment, so take your time and do it right.

Bird Fairs

In many towns, bird fairs begin to pop up about the same time as the trees begin to bud in spring. These fairs are usually (but not always) sponsored by local bird clubs, and feature an array of birds, cages, toys and supplies, and bird-related jewelry and such. Bird fairs often bring together a wide selection of birds, and offer potential buyers a chance to speak with local breeders. There's usually a festival-like atmosphere, and they're a great place for looking, learning, buying supplies, and socializing. But in my opinion, they're a lousy place to buy a bird. Okay, that's a little harsh, but here's the problem: If just one bird in the entire exhibition hall is carrying a contagious disease, then every bird in that facility is potentially exposed. The birds are crowded, probably stressed, and are exposed to not only other birds, but to

hundreds of strangers passing by and poking and prodding at their cage.

Years ago, I belonged to a bird club that held frequent fairs. One year, a woman brought in a cockatiel that "had the sniffles." Our club was very careful about checking out any birds on display, and we even had an avian veterinarian on hand to visually inspect all birds before they entered and deny admission to those that looked ill. But somehow, this cockatiel remained under everyone's radar. Within a week, I began

How to Spot a Sick Bird

Although it's possible for a conure to appear perfectly healthy while harboring disease, there are usually signs—sometimes subtle—that should cause you to steer clear. Begin by evaluating the bird from a distance. Conures are prey animals, which means that a sick or injured individual could be easy pickings for a hungry predator. As such, weakened birds will typically use all their strength to appear normal and keep up with the flock. By the time a parrot is showing obvious signs of sickness, it is probably gravely ill and too weakened to maintain the facade. By observing from a distance, you'll often be able to pick up more subtle signs because the bird has let its guard down, thinking that no one (meaning no potential predator) is watching.

✔ Sick birds are usually less active than healthy ones. A conure that appears lethargic, disinterested in its surroundings, or excessively sleepy might be ill. Note that baby birds tend to sleep more than adults, but a healthy yet sleepy parrot will usually snap to attention if something catches its interest. Also, sleepy birds, like sleepy humans, tend to yawn a lot. Absence of yawning might be a tip-off that something other than a lack of sleep is causing the lethargy.

✔ Ruffled feathers and partially closed eyes can also mean either sleepy or sick. A bird that's cold, tired, or sick will puff out its feathers to trap body heat and keep warm. A healthy conure preparing for a nap usually yawns, stretches, and pulls one foot up into its feathers, perching on the other one. Its eyes might be heavy, but they're clear and quick to focus on nearby movements. An ill bird usually slouches on the perch with both feet, and its droopy eyes might appear watery or unfocused. And, although baby birds often sleep on the cage floor even after they're

capable of perching, an adult bird that refuses to perch and sits on the cage floor is likely very ill.

✔ A healthy bird's breathing is nearly indiscernible: there's no sound, and only the slightest rise and fall of the chest or abdomen. A conure that's been romping and wrestling with a cagemate or toy might be breathing a little heavier, but the breath is smooth and unlabored. A sick bird, on the other hand, might wheeze, rattle, or click as it struggles to breathe. The bird's tail might pump up and down with each breath as it struggles to move air in and out of its lungs. Also, any type of discharge from the nares (nostrils) is a probable sign of disease.

✔ Smooth, brilliant feathers are one of the surest signs of good health in a parrot. However, feathers can be damaged or unsightly even in an otherwise healthy bird. Baby birds especially are clumsy, rowdy, and sometimes lacking in personal hygiene skills. If the conure you're considering has some feather issues, take a look at its surroundings. Does it have a cagemate that might be causing damage? I've often seen playful babies play tug-of-war with each other's tail feathers. Tail and flight feathers can also get broken if the cage is too small or too crowded with toys. Conures love to roll around and lie on their backs, so bits of debris might be wedged in the feathers until bath time. If there's no obvious explanation for the damage, proceed with caution. An adult bird with frayed, pulled, or chewed feathers can be suffering from a wide array of illnesses, behavioral problems, or nutritional deficiencies. Clubbed or deformed feathers in a parrot of any age can signify deadly viruses. If you're unsure, walk away.

✔ If possible, take a close look at the bird's droppings. (You might as well get used to it now—once you own a pet bird, droppings will become an integral part of your life!) Healthy

parrot droppings consist of three parts: dark green or brownish tubular feces, white pasty urates, and clear urine. Unlike excretion from carnivorous mammals, parrot droppings usually have little or no odor. In a textbook-perfect dropping, all three parts are present and clearly discernable. A bird that's nervous, or one who has drunk a lot of water or eaten watery food, might produce a very loose dropping with lots of urine yet few urates and feces. This is known as "polyuria," and it's usually transient and nothing to worry about. Chronic polyuria can signify metabolic diseases, especially diabetes, but would usually be combined with other symptoms such as weight loss. Polyuria is not to be confused with diarrhea, in which the feces are poorly formed, sometimes smelly, and discolored. Diarrhea always signals that something is amiss; transient polyuria rarely does. Keep in mind that baby birds being fed a liquid formula might have softer less-formed stools, and certain foods such as berries and beets can discolor the droppings tremendously for a short time after eating. Egg-laying hens might also produce somewhat smelly and voluminous droppings, but it is not the same as diarrhea. If you see signs of diarrhea, discolored droppings that can't be explained by diet (especially green- or yellow-tinged urates), or undigested food in the droppings, do not purchase the bird—it is probably ill.

✔ A healthy conure is of good weight—not too skinny or too fat. A baby bird might be a little pudgy until it's fully weaned and adjusted to an adult diet, but an overweight adult bird is subject to the same obesity-related diseases as obese humans: diabetes, cardiovascular disease, and respiratory problems. A bird that's too thin (assuming it hasn't been abused and underfed) is probably burning up calories fighting an under-lying disease. There are a few ways to determine healthy weight in a parrot. You can weigh the bird and compare its weight to known healthy ranges for its species. Of course, this doesn't take into account individual variances. Once you own the bird, regular weigh-ins will allow you to establish a weight range that's healthy and normal for your particular pet. Due to their relatively small size, parrot weights are almost always given in grams for the sake of accuracy. You can purchase a bird scale complete with perch, but an inexpensive electronic postal or kitchen scale works just fine, as long as it converts to grams. If you don't have a scale handy, or don't know the proper weight for a species, you can get a pretty accurate idea by examining the keel bone (also called the breast bone) that runs down the center of a bird's chest. A fat bird will have "cleavage," which is muscle tissue bulging up on either side of the keel. A thin bird will have a prominent keel bone, with a tent-like appearance as the muscle falls away from the bone rapidly on either side. The chest can appear sunken on each side of the keel. In a bird of healthy weight, the keel bone will be almost invisible, with healthy muscle creating a gently rounded and smooth chest.

getting frantic phone calls from breeders whose birds had fallen ill—a few even died. By comparing the sick birds with a layout of our vendor booths, we soon honed in on the source of the outbreak: one little snuffly cockatiel, which turned out to be carrying *Chlamydiosis,* also known as psittacosis or parrot fever. This is a disease that is reportable to local health authorities, and requires rigorous treatment and quarantine for affected birds. It can also be passed on to humans. Needless to say, it was a nightmare for everyone involved.

If you see a bird fair in your neighborhood, by all means visit, ask questions, collect phone numbers, or buy supplies. If you meet a conure breeder you like, you can always arrange to visit his or her home at a future date. Just be very cautious about buying any bird that has very recently been on public display. Having said all this, there have been a few times when I haven't followed my own advice, and I've purchased birds directly from fairs. I do, however, strictly quarantine the new arrival, and so far I've been lucky. The point is, buying a parrot that has been exposed to other birds in this manner does greatly increase your risk of getting a sick bird, and is probably not the best way to acquire your first pet.

The Internet

In this electronic age, a new pet conure might just be a few clicks away on your computer. If you're looking for a specific species that isn't available in your area, this can be a valid solution. Although shipping birds across the country is a necessary and common method for breeders to obtain stock, I would consider it a last resort for someone looking for a pet. Shipping adds a layer of risk and expense to the transaction that isn't necessary just to obtain a pet. You might, however, find a seller that is willing to drive a reasonable distance and meet you halfway. I've completed many parrot purchases and sales at interstate truck stops in my day, and it saves hundreds of dollars in shipping costs, not to mention that a pleasurable car ride with a familiar person is probably much less stressful for the bird than being tossed in the cargo compartment of an airplane. Use extreme caution in long-distance purchases, however, because there are some unethical or downright fraudulent people selling sick birds, or scamming deposit money and then disappearing behind Internet aliases. There are two well-known Internet sites for bird lovers that do a fairly good job of policing their advertisers: upatsix.com and birdsnways.com. Upatsix.com allows users to post feedback on sellers, so you can benefit from other folks' experiences.

Health Guarantees

Before you purchase your conure, always ask the sellers about their health guarantees. Pet stores often have a formal written guarantee, while breeders might have a more loose agreement. Don't assume that the seller will take back or reimburse you for a sick or dead bird—a few sellers guarantee only "alive on delivery." That's usually the exception, and most reputable places will offer some kind of health guarantee, but be certain to ask (and understand) the terms and limitations up front. Most of these agreements have some type of provision that requires a veterinary exam within a certain period of time after purchase—commonly 48 hours—or the agreement is void. This is to insure that the bird was healthy when it was delivered to you, and to protect the seller in case your abuse or neglect cause the parrot to quickly fall ill under your care.

Preparing for the New Arrival

Before you bring your conure home, you'll need to prepare for its arrival. In advance, purchase a suitable cage and all needed supplies, including food, toys, and treats. Check with the seller to see what type of food the bird is eating, and have some on hand. Get the cage set up and situated properly. The last thing in the world you want to do is bring home a parrot without advance preparations! Your new pet will be stressed enough; please don't add to its stress by letting it sit in a small travel carrier in a strange home while you try to decipher cage assembly instructions. The following chapter will cover in detail all you'll need to know about cages and other conure doodads.

Transporting

Okay, you've found the perfect conure—now how do you get it home? I suggest purchasing an appropriately sized pet carrier, such as the common "pet taxis" sold for cats and dogs.

These hard plastic carriers usually have a front wire grate that your bird can hold onto during transit. Don't think of it as a one-time need. It will get plenty of use for veterinary visits, family travel, and evacuation safety. I wouldn't recommend trying to transport your conure in the flimsy cardboard boxes that pet stores usually provide as transport. Even the smallest conure species have strong hooked beaks, and cardboard won't hold an antsy parrot for very long. You really don't want a frightened parrot thrashing loose around your car on the drive home. Trust me.

Finding an Avian Veterinarian

The best time to find an avian veterinarian is before you bring your conure home. Making frantic phone calls when a sick or injured bird is lying on the cage floor is a really bad time to start looking. And please don't think that you can just bring your conure to the veterinarian who cares for your dog and cat. Most small mammal vets see few birds, and have little experience dealing with parrots. Your best choice, if you can find one, is a veterinarian that specializes in birds, and has been board-certified in avian medicine by the American Board of Veterinary Practitioners (AVMP). Unless you live near a large city or near a veterinary college, however, these specialists can be hard to find. More realistically, look for a practitioner that sees a lot of birds, and is preferably a member of the Association of Avian Veterinarians (AAV). Although AAV membership isn't a guarantee of expertise, it at least indicates that the doctor has a strong interest in avian clients, and is attempting to stay current on new research and treatment options. You can contact the AAV at (561) 393-8901 or visit their website at www.aav.org for a list of member vets in your area. Local bird breeders and pet stores can also recommend qualified practitioners, and sometimes a recommendation from someone with personal experience is worth more than all the fancy initials after a name.

The First Veterinarian Visit

As mentioned earlier, some sellers require that you bring your bird to a veterinarian in order to activate the health guarantee. Whether or not this is the case, the first vet visit is extremely important for many reasons. Most obviously, the veterinarian will examine your conure for any subtle signs of diseases or disorders that you might not have noticed. Dealing with trouble early in parrots can often be the difference between life and death. More than likely your pet will be perfectly healthy, but a routine physical exam, weigh-in, and perhaps a blood analysis and bacterial culture or stain will give you and the doctor a normal baseline to measure against for the rest of the bird's life. The first exam is also a wonderful time to ask questions about care or any other concerns you might have. Of course you don't want to waste a busy veterinarian's time with dozens of simple questions that could be answered with some basic research, but feel free to bring a list of questions that merit an expert's advice. There are several tests your veterinarian might recommend to rule out dangerous diseases, and these recommendations might depend on whether or not you own other birds. (See the chapter on Health and Disease for an in-depth discussion of disease risks for your conure.)

Quarantine

If you have any other birds at home, it's critical to quarantine the new arrival until it's reasonably certain that it's not carrying any communicable diseases. Many dangerous diseases can exist in a sub-clinical state, which means your new pet might be a carrier even though it is showing no symptoms. Proper testing can rule out some of these diseases, but not all. Your veterinarian can advise on the length of quarantine necessary, but it's typically 30 to 60 days. Unfortunately, it's nearly impossible to perform a complete quarantine in an average household—shared airflow, traffic from people and other pets, and a host of other issues will compromise the procedure—but some common sense cautions will go a long way towards protecting your other birds. Of course, if the newcomer is your only bird, quarantine is unnecessary.

The First Days at Home

Once you get your conure home and settled into its cage, give it some time to get used to its new surroundings. Limit visitors, and don't allow family members to crowd or harass the bird. It is of course human nature to want to cuddle and play with the new pet, but even a very tame conure will feel a bit nervous and overloaded in a new home. Think of how you might feel when you arrive at an exotic vacation locale: excited and happy, but perhaps a little jet-lagged and overwhelmed. Let the bird have a bite to eat, then have a restful afternoon and a good night's sleep. Take your cues from the bird's behavior. If it's active and begging for attention, feel free to cuddle. If it's withdrawn and quiet, talk softly to it and spend some time in the same room, but don't

Common Sense Quarantine

Temporarily situate your new conure in a spare room or other area of your home as far away as possible from existing pet birds. Be aware that other cage bird species, such as finches, canaries, and doves, can still transmit or fall victim to many of the same diseases that affect conures.

Feed and clean the new conure last, after all your other pets have been serviced. Before and after you enter the quarantine area, wash your hands thoroughly. For that matter, get in the habit of washing your hands carefully before and after you handle any pet—bird, mammal, or reptile. Humans are frequent carriers of several nasty strains of bacteria, so bacterial contamination can be a hazard to both you and your pet. A little hygiene will help keep everyone healthy.

Try to limit traffic from people and pets into and out of the quarantine area. Germs can easily hitch a ride on clothing and shoes, or on your dog or cat's fur and paws.

If you have forced air heating and cooling, consider closing the vents in the quarantine room and cracking open a window for fresh air if weather permits.

Don't use the same sponge, broom, or mop between rooms, or you'll just be carrying possible pathogens throughout the house. If this isn't feasible, at least rinse your cleaning tools between areas and use a suitable disinfectant. (See page 35 for more information on disinfectants.)

force it to come out and interact until it's ready. With lots of love and good care, you'll have a whole lifetime together; there's no need to rush.

Before you bring your conure home, you'll need to set up a safe and secure haven for your new pet.

Okay, you've done all your research and found the perfect bird. Now what? Obviously a proper cage is important, but cage placement and environmental factors must figure into your decision as well. A tame bird will be lonely and bored in a dark deserted corner. On the other hand, it will probably suffer from perpetual stress if its cage is plopped dead center in the middle of the family's bustling high-traffic zone. Please don't bring a conure home until you've purchased the cage and supplies and have everything set up and ready in a well thought out spot. A little advance preparation will go a long way in easing the transition for everyone involved, especially for the new arrival.

Types of Cages

Bird cages come in a dizzying array of sizes, colors, shapes, price ranges, and materials.

Hawk-headed parrots (Deroptyus accipitrinus) share many features and traits with Pyrrhura conures, but are classed as an entirely separate breed.

Some are basic and utilitarian, while others are designed to look like fine furniture. Your taste and budget will narrow the choices, but you should still find plenty from which to choose. Remember that your final decision not only impacts your bird's comfort and welfare, but will also dictate how much time and effort you spend on upkeep. The ideal cage will give your conure plenty of room for safe play and rest, yet it will be easy to care for and clean.

Cage Shape and Design

The best cage shapes for conures are rectangular or square with flat barred roofs. Most conures love to hang upside down and do battle with their toys, so avoid solid metal or plastic roofs that prevent this type of healthy exercise and play. Don't choose round or pagoda-shaped cages either, because these shapes are not "user-friendly" for parrots. Many birds display anxiety in round cages, probably because there's no safe corner in which to retreat. Odd shapes such as pagodas can have lots of poorly utilized spaces that

Greater Patagonians are the largest species of conure.

make them harder to clean yet offer the bird less actual room to play. Also try to avoid peaked or domed roofs that make hanging toys and swings more difficult and limit the bird's ability to climb about.

Some authors recommend buying cages with mostly horizontal bars so that the bird can climb with ease, but I've yet to meet a conure that was incapable of scaling vertical bars. The true benefit of bar direction is for the owners: vertical bars are less likely to collect poop, and are therefore easier to clean. It's unlikely to

make a difference to your conure, so don't put too much weight on that feature.

Cage Sizing

For a small conure such as a Green-cheeked or Dusky, the cage should be at least 18 inches (46 cm) square and 20 to 25 inches (51–63.5 cm) high. Nandays, Jendays, and other medium-sized conures require a cage about 24 inches (61 cm) square, and large conures such as Blue-crowned and Patagonians need even more room, perhaps 30 inches (76 cm) wide and 24 inches (61 cm) deep. As a rule of thumb, choose a cage that's at least 1½ times the length of the bird's wingspan. In other words, if your conure has a wingspan of 16 inches (41 cm), it should be housed in a cage that is at least 24 inches (61 cm) wide: 16 × 1.5 = 24. Anything smaller will not allow the bird enough room to play, flap, and exercise, and can invite behavioral problems from stress.

You can certainly go larger, but use common sense. A too-large cage might make the bird feel insecure and unprotected, so don't place a single bird in a floor-to-ceiling aviary unless you provide a roosting area that it can retreat to for a sense of safety. Parrots are territorial, and that would be a lot of turf to defend! If you're housing a pair of conures, the cage should be large enough to allow each occupant enough room to have some personal quiet time when desired.

Bar Spacing

Bar spacing is an important factor to consider in terms of safety. If the bars are spaced too far apart, there is a risk that your conure will stick its head between the bars and get stuck. It's easy for a curious parrot to push for-ward through the bars, but not at all as easy for a frightened and struggling bird to pull back its head against the lay of its feathers. Even if it doesn't get stuck, it will temporarily be much more vulnerable to other household pets.

On the other hand, cages with extremely nar-row bar spacing are likely intended for smaller soft bill birds such as canaries and finches, and the bars may not be strong enough to with-stand the beak strength of a parrot. If you can wiggle the bars easily with your fingers, it's likely your conure will bend or wiggle them until the welds break. Look for sturdy medium gauge wire with a spacing of $1/2$ inch (1.3 cm) to $5/8$ inch (1.6 cm) between the bars for small conures, and up to $3/4$ inch (1.9 cm) spacing for the larger species. Most reputable cage compa-nies do a good job of matching up bar spacing and cage sizing for the intended sizes of occu-pants, but there are unfortunately quite a few poorly designed cages (mostly cheap imports) on the market.

Cage Materials

There are plenty of cage materials on the market to choose from, but not all of them are really suitable for pet birds. Some are made with potentially toxic materials, and others are safe but difficult to clean. Never buy a birdcage designed for decorative use only, because these are not intended for live birds and will likely contain dangerous amounts of lead or other toxic metals. Do not buy any cages made with bamboo or wooden bars, because your conure will promptly chew it to splinters, and these materials are nearly impossible to clean and disinfect. I also recommend against antique

cages for many of the same reasons. We now understand much more about metal toxicity in birds than they did in previous decades, so old cages might not be safe, and will likely be hard to clean to boot. Even newer used cages can be problematic if the previous occupant died from an infectious disease that is still lurking in the cage's cracks and crevices.

Your best bet for cleaning and safety is a new, high quality plated wire or powder coated wrought iron design. Avoid galvanized or painted wire, because these can be a source of lead or unacceptable levels of zinc. I also rec-ommend avoiding cages with plastic bases and trays, because these tend to dry out, crack, and warp over time, and aren't really designed to withstand the beak assault of a playful conure.

The Zinc Controversy

Over the past several years, a debate has raged in the avicultural community about the role of zinc in a bird's health. Zinc is a necessary trace mineral that enhances immune function and aids in cell generation and wound healing. In large amounts, however, it is toxic, and can lead to a variety of health problems. Almost all metal cages and cage accessories, with the exception of stainless steel, contain varying amounts of zinc. Zinc is also present in certain rubber toys, fortified foods, and a host of other products that your bird might come in contact with.

In the earlier days of aviculture, folks noticed that birds kept in new galvanized wire cages, and those using galvanized feed and water dishes, often displayed a constellation of symp-toms (including gastrointestinal problems and seizures) that became known as "new wire disease." Oddly enough, birds housed in older galvanized cages didn't seem to be affected. Researchers discovered that the manufacturing process for galvanized wire left a large amount of free zinc on the wire surface, and parrots living in these cages could ingest toxic levels of the mineral when the wire was new. Over time, the surface zinc either washed away or became bonded to the wire so that the exposure was greatly reduced. The zinc was still there, but not in a form that was likely to be easily ingested. Most bird keepers began scrubbing down new wire with a mildly acidic mixture of vinegar and water, which was reasonably effective at

removing or bonding free zinc, and new wire disease was largely forgotten.

In recent years, however, some researchers have questioned what, if any, effect environmental zinc has on the health of captive birds. The topic is somewhat contentious, and much of the research is conflicting. Although you should obviously protect your pet from exposure to the high levels of zinc that can leach from galvanized cups or unscrubbed galvanized wire, it's less clear if any danger exists from plated metal cages or metal toy parts. I personally feel comfortable housing my birds in good quality plated or powder-coated cages, and I've done random blood testing on my flock to check for any elevated blood zinc levels, which have never been a problem. If you have any concerns, discuss the issue with your avian veterinarian for advice or blood testing protocols.

Cage Placement

Once you find the perfect cage for your new pet, you'll need to find the right spot for your bird to live in your home. Actually, as mentioned at the beginning of this chapter, I recommend deciding on cage placement before you even begin shopping so that you can insure a good fit and enough room for properly servicing the cage. Parrots are social creatures and need to be part of your "flock" activity to be happy. Please don't purchase a pet conure unless you're willing and able to make it an integral part of your family.

What, then, is the most suitable spot? Kitchens are usually a poor choice because cooking fumes and cleaning chemicals can pose a threat to a parrot's delicate respiratory system. Bedrooms aren't ideal unless you're the

Household Hazards

The household can be a minefield of dangers to a parrot. Be aware of the following:

✔ Other pets pose a serious threat to an unsupervised bird. Cats, dogs, ferrets and snakes are all predators and should never be trusted around an uncaged or poorly caged bird. Larger parrots can seriously injure or kill your conure should they become territorial or jealous. Even smaller parrots can deliver a nasty bite if a curious conure ventures too close.

✔ Open water containers such as toilets, mop buckets, and aquariums are drowning hazards. Parrots do not have the same waterproofing on their feathers as ducks and geese do, and a waterlogged conure probably will not be able to escape a water-filled container. Even a water glass can trap a curious pet.

✔ Ceiling fans can kill a flighted bird. Keep your conure's wings clipped, and turn off fans whenever your pet is out.

✔ Some household fumes will sicken or kill pet birds due to their delicate respiratory system. Avoid aerosol products or products with harsh fumes, including but not limited to lacquers, paint thinners, oven cleaners, and room deodorizers. If you must, only use them in a well-ventilated area and temporarily move your birds to a safer part of the house. When in doubt, always err on the side of caution. Non-toxic products are safer for your bird *and* your family.

✔ Teflon is a ubiquitous chemical coating used in non-stick pans, stove burners, irons and ironing board covers, some heat lamps, and many other products. When overheated it produces an odorless colorless gas known as polytetrafluoroethylene (PTFE) that is deadly to birds. Even normal usage has the potential to emit low-level fumes. An exposed bird will usually die immediately, although some birds with minor exposure can survive with immediate fresh air and quick veterinary treatment. These fumes can also cause mild flu-like illness in humans. If you keep birds, I recommend switching to safer types of cookware, such as stainless steel or anodized aluminum. There have also been reports of pet birds dying from the fumes produced when self-cleaning ovens are operated in the high-heat cleaning mode, so consider scrubbing your oven the old-fashioned way.

✔ Lists of poisonous plants are available online but are sometimes incomplete or inaccurate. Just don't let your bird chew on any houseplants! Your plants will look better, and your conure will be safer. Keep a list handy of the scientific and common names of any plants you keep in the home, so if your bird does chomp its way through your *Saintpaulia ionantha* (African violet—generally considered non-toxic) you can call the Animal Poison Information Center at (800) 548-2423 and they'll tell you not to worry.

✔ Most toxic substances in the house might be obvious, but others will surprise you. For example, chocolate, avocado, caffeine, and nicotine are all poisonous to birds. Parrots are like toddlers, and will put a variety of substances in their mouths. It's up to you as the adult to monitor them and keep them safe from harm.

✔ People are also a danger to birds. Not intentionally, of course, but all too often pet parrots are accidentally killed by being stepped on, sat on, or crushed in a door. Always be aware of your conure's location when it's out of its cage, and don't let pet birds play on the floor unattended where they're the most vulnerable. And never allow your conure to nap with you. If you fall asleep, you run the risk of suffocating or crushing your pet if you roll onto it.

type who actually enjoys being awakened at the crack of dawn by an exuberant bird greeting the sun each morning. The ideal spot is usually a living room or den where family members gather when at home. Place the cage in a spot where the bird can oversee all the activity while remaining out of reach of romping dogs and tussling children. Your conure will want to participate in family fun, but from a safe vantage point.

Always make sure the cage is on a sturdy stand to prevent it from accidentally being knocked over, and place it high enough to protect the bird from the probing noses and paws of other pets. Your conure might enjoy being placed near a window so that it can watch the outside birds, but be sure that it has a shaded area to retreat to if the sun's rays get too warm. Although conures generally are hardy birds, your pet will appreciate being protected from drafts and extreme temperature changes, so try to avoid placing the cage too close to heating and air conditioning vents.

Perches and Other Cage Accessories

Perches are sort of like footwear for birds. Just as too-tight shoes can cause you discomfort and pain, the wrong perches can cause foot pain and pressure sores in parrots. The typical round dowel perches that are supplied with many cages are the worst offenders; the smooth and uniform diameter does not allow the bird's foot to flex normally and redistribute weight. It's fine to leave one of these perches in the cage for convenience, but always add additional styles and textures to give your pet's feet a healthy workout.

Perch Materials

Suitable perches are now available in many different materials, and your conure will enjoy a mixture of types.

✔ Natural branch perches made of cleaned and dried woods such as manzanita, grapevine, and driftwood are available in an assortment of sizes and diameters. These are ideal, because the varying thicknesses and angles of natural branches exercise the foot muscles, improve balance, and create a more natural environment for your conure. You can also gather appropriately sized tree branches from your backyard, but scrub them thoroughly with hot soapy water, rinse well, and dry completely before using them to avoid possible disease transmission from outdoor birds. To be completely safe, you can bake them in a low oven—set at 200°F (93°C)—for an hour or so which will kill almost all pathogens. Most trees are safe, but avoid "stone fruit" trees (such as cherry, peach, and nectarine) and yew, which are highly toxic if your parrot chews them. Check with your veterinarian or local U.S. Department of Agriculture Cooperative Extension office for advice on the safety of specific tree species. And, of course, never gather branches from trees that have been sprayed with pesticides, or from trees near roadways that are subject to high levels of automobile exhaust.

✔ "Pedicure perches" include a wide variety of abrasive materials that are intended to gradually and gently wear down a bird's toenails with regular use. These perches are commonly made of concrete, terra cotta, or sand-coated hardwood. They provide a sturdy non-slip surface, and birds will also use them to wipe their beaks and remove flaky patches. Some folks have voiced concern that they're too rough for tender feet, but my experience has shown just the opposite. My birds actually prefer these perches over other styles, and I believe regular use keeps their feet soft and supple.

✔ Rope perches are soft and bendable, and provide a gentle and cushioned surface for playing or sleeping. The problems with rope perches are that they are difficult to clean thoroughly, and as they wear and fray the fibers can pose a danger if a bird becomes entangled. They're still a nice option, but inspect them frequently and replace them when they become dirty or worn.

✔ Acrylic or PVC plastic perches became very popular several years ago, because they're easy to clean and practically indestructible. Unfortunately, they're frequently slippery for the bird and are typically manufactured in a uniform diameter like the wooden dowel perches. It's fine to add one of these to your bird's cage for variety, but these types should never be used as the only perches in a cage.

Remember, variety is the key, so offer your pet a mix of styles and textures to keep its feet and joints healthy and well exercised.

Food and Water Cups

In addition to perches, properly furnished cages require a variety of food, water, and treat cups. It's likely that some will be supplied with the cage, but they might not be the best choice for safety and ease of cleaning. Even if they are, you should purchase duplicate (or even triplicate) sets so that you're never without clean dishes to service the cage. You can simply toss

the dirty set into the dishwasher or into the sink to soak, and replace with the clean backup set.

When you're choosing cups, look for sturdy styles that are easy to clean and non-reactive with foods. I personally prefer stainless steel or heavy ceramic crocks, but be aware that once ceramic chips or cracks it can create a breeding ground for bacteria. Replace worn cups as needed. Galvanized metal and some low-quality imported ceramics can react with liquids or acidic foods and leach lead, zinc, or other toxic metals. Heavy-duty plastic cups are fine, but they will crack and discolor easily, and your conure will likely gnaw them to bits if they're a

The Fiery-shouldered (or Demerara) conure (**Pyrrhura egregia**) *is uncommon in aviculture, but a few breeders occasionally have chicks for sale.*

The Cuban Conure (**Aratinga euops**) *is uncommon in aviculture, and is sometime mistaken for the more common White-eyed conure.*

lightweight plastic. You might want to purchase a variety and see which ones suit your needs the best. Allow at least three dishes per cage: one for water, one for dry food (pellets and seed), and one for fresh or cooked foods.

Other Cage Accessories

In order to remain healthy and happy, your conure will require a lot of sleep—about ten hours a night or more. The best way to ensure that your pet has plenty of quality snooze time is to provide a cage cover. A cage cover can be a fancy custom item made to fit the cage's exact dimension, or it can be a simple piece of heavy dark fabric that is large enough to drape over the entire cage. Twin size flat bed sheets in a dark solid color are inexpensive, easy to wash, and simple to replace when they get chewed or worn. Light colored fabrics won't block enough light, and vibrant color patterns might be upsetting to your pet, so stick with solid black, dark blue, or dark forest green.

Another accessory you might consider is a seed apron or "mess catcher." Like all parrots, conures are usually messy and exuberant eaters. They will toss seed, fling fruit, splash water, and generally create havoc with their food. To thwart or at least reduce this behavior, several companies have designed panels that attach to the outside of the cage and funnel the mess back inside the cage. I don't find them particularly helpful, because I think it is easier to clean the food off the floor (or let the dog do it) than it is to scrub the aprons, but some folks swear by them.

Travel Cages

In addition to its permanent cage, your conure should have a small travel cage for trips to the vet, emergency evacuations, and other short trips. A travel cage can be a regular bird cage in a smaller size, just large enough to house your pet temporarily, or it can be one of the plastic "pet taxis" mentioned in the second chapter of this book. I like the pet taxis with a front grate. These are usually slotted or perforated plastic boxes with a wire or plastic grate door on the front and a carrying handle on top. The mostly solid sides keep the carrier dark and give the bird a sense of security, but the front grate allows it to see what's happening. They're easy to carry, and easy to clean and disinfect. Just be certain the brand you choose is sturdy and durable, because conures can eventually chew through cheap plastic and escape.

Once you have a travel cage, I recommend setting up a birdie emergency kit for your pet. Purchase a waterproof pouch that will fit inside the carrier, and keep a container of bird food, some bottled water, dishes for food and water, hand sanitizer, contact information for your veterinarian, and a towel (for warmth or for restraining an injured bird) inside the pouch, and place it into the carrier. If you are forced to evacuate your home due to a sudden emergency such as fire, flood, or other disaster, you can quickly place your bird in the carrier and evacuate it safely with the rest of the family.

Lighting and Air Quality

Now that you've gotten the inside of the cage all figured out, it's time to give some thought to the surrounding environment. Just like people, birds thrive on fresh air and sunshine. Because both of these are in short supply inside the average house, you'll need to improvise.

The Right Light

Birds—just like plants, animals, and people—use the sun's rays for a variety of metabolic processes, including vitamin synthesis. For example, vitamin D is produced through a chemical reaction when sunlight touches the skin. Sunlight is composed of a wide spectrum of both visible and invisible rays ranging from infrared up through ultraviolet. Regular incandescent lighting contains almost no ultraviolet, and is also lacking on the blue end of

the light spectrum. Standard fluorescent bulbs are a little better, but they're still a poor substitute for sunlight. Therefore, parrots housed indoors without access to the necessary ultraviolet rays can be deficient in vitamin D, which the body needs to properly utilize calcium.

To keep your conure healthy, you'll need to provide a daily source of full-spectrum light. Placing your bird's cage in front of a window won't help, because window glass and plastic filter about 99 percent of the ultraviolet spectrum. The best alternative is to purchase a full-spectrum light to position near the cage. Full-spectrum bulbs fit standard light fixtures, and they're designed to mimic the sun's rays as closely as possible. Once hard to find, these bulbs are now widely available at pet shops, home supply stores, craft stores, and on the Internet. Do not purchase light bulbs marketed for reptile use, because these are designed for the very different light spectrum needs of reptile species only, and may actually be detrimental to your conure's health. Make sure the bulb says "full-spectrum" or "mimics natural sunlight." Some well-respected brands include Chromalux, Verilux, Ott Lights, and Vita-Lites.

Most birds will do well with ten to fourteen hours of artificial daylight each day, but make sure your pet has at least ten hours of darkness and quiet for quality sleep. Light exerts a powerful influence on living creatures, and can affect your bird's hormones, health, and mood. If you're uncertain, check with your avian veterinarian for advice.

Air Quality

Indoor air quality is important not just for the health of your bird, but also for your health and that of other family members. Due in part to a lack of proper air flow, the air inside a well-insulated home can be a veritable cesspool of bacteria, viruses, fungi, dust, chemical pollutants, and other irritants. Your conure will contribute its feather dander and aerosolized feces to this mix, which can aggravate allergies and asthma in susceptible individuals. Fresh air from open windows is a wonderful antidote, but not always a practical solution during cold weather or peak allergen seasons.

If tossing open a window isn't always an option, or if the air quality in your community leaves something to be desired, consider adding an air purification system to your home. Air purifiers range from complicated and pricey whole-house systems down to portable individual desktop versions. The most important factors are how much air the system can process, and how the air is processed.

The most effective type uses HEPA filtration, which is an acronym for high efficiency particulate air filtration. HEPA filters were designed by scientists from the Manhattan Project in the 1940s, for the purpose of removing radioactive particles from the air. HEPA filters remove at least 99.97 percent of airborne particles, so they're invaluable in fields such as medicine, nuclear technology, computer chip manufacturing, and anywhere else that air quality is critical. Of course, they're also great for cleansing the air in your home and making you and your family safer and more comfortable. Many manufacturers combine HEPA filters with inexpensive washable or disposable carbon prefilters to prolong the life of the HEPA filter and make its use more economical.

The other important factor in choosing an air purifier is determining the proper size for the intended use. Air cleaners are typically rated by how many cubic feet of air they can process in a minute, or CFM. The higher the CFM, the more effective the purifier. A high CFM unit won't remove any more particles than a low CFM unit, but it will do so faster and more efficiently. Always be certain that the unit you choose is rated for the size of the room in which you wish to use it, or you might be disappointed with the

Nanday conures are commonly kept as pets.

results. And, to maintain performance and efficiency, always clean and replace the filters as recommended by the manufacturer.

Cleaning the Cage

Although clean air is vitally important, it won't do much to keep your conure healthy if your pet is wallowing in a filthy cage. As I've said, parrots are messy creatures that require a certain amount of upkeep to maintain. In my experience, it's much easier to do a little cleaning each day than it is to wait until the dried droppings require a hammer and chisel to remove them. If you break the job down to daily, weekly, and "as needed" tasks, cage cleaning will require little effort.

Daily Tasks

✔ Replace and refill food and water dishes. Never "top off" food dishes because they appear partially full. Parrots hull seed before eating it, so what appears to be a full dish of seed might actually be a dish filled with empty seed hulls. Even when food remains, both seed and formulated diets can become stale and rancid when exposed to air, light, and moisture. Always supply fresh food and water daily!

✔ Replace cage bottom paper. I don't recommend cage substrates such as pine shavings, ground corncob, or sand because they are messy and can harbor dangerous pathogens if not changed frequently. Although they look neat, substrates will add greatly to the expense and upkeep of the cage. I use custom-sized Cage Catchers brand cage papers (see Resource Guide), but any plain paper or newsprint will work just fine. Newspapers are printed with non-toxic inks, so they pose no danger should your bird ingest them. Just avoid glossy paper

Suggested Cleaning Kit
- A sturdy plastic tote to carry supplies
- Broom and dustpan
- Scrub brushes
- Paper towels
- Soft cloth for cleaning and drying. (New cloth diapers or microfiber work great.)
- Textured scrub sponge
- Spray bottle filled with water
- White vinegar
- Baking soda
- Enzymatic cleaners such as Poop-Off, or other non-toxic cleaner.

stock, which is likely to be coated with undesirable chemicals.

✔ Sweep around the cage. Molted feathers and food debris are attractive bait for insects and rodents. Daily vigilance can help you avoid a future pest problem.

Weekly Tasks

✔ Wipe down the cage bars with a damp soft cloth. Plain water is fine, or you can add a splash of white vinegar or dish soap to enhance the cleaning power. For spots that need a bit more scrubbing, make a paste of baking soda with a little water for a safe and gentle abrasive. There are also safe and non-toxic enzymatic products on the market that will quickly and effectively dissolve dried-on droppings or food. One such product is Poop-Off, and it is widely available in pet stores and on the Internet.

✔ Remove any perches and toys that show an accumulation of crud. Scrape off what you can, and soak or scrub thoroughly with hot water. Replace any that are frayed, worn, or broken.

Fiery-shouldered conures are relatively common in their natural range, but not well established in captive breeding programs.

Remove cage trays and grates and scrub. Dry thoroughly before replacing.

As-Needed Tasks

How often you will need to perform these tasks will depend on the number of birds you keep, what (if any) illnesses are circulating among your birds, and how thoroughly you've performed daily and weekly maintenance. In general, once a year might be sufficient for a pet bird or two, but aviaries containing multiple pairs might require seasonal or even more frequent attention. Begin by removing your conure from the cage and placing it in its travel cage in a safe location. Be sure to provide some food and water.

✔ Remove all perches, toys, and cage accessories and inspect them carefully. Discard any damaged or excessively worn items, or porous items (including fabric toys and wooden nest boxes) that can't be properly disinfected.

✔ Scrub the remaining accessories in hot soapy water and rinse carefully. Certain items, especially hardwood perches and plastic toys, can safely be run through your dishwasher to clean and disinfect.

✔ Scrub the cage thoroughly with hot soapy water and a bristled brush or scrubby sponge. You can place a small cage in the bathtub, or drag a larger one outside to rinse with a garden hose or pressure washer. Rinse and dry completely.

✔ Disinfect as needed.

Disinfection

If your birds have been exposed to any contagious diseases, you'll want to disinfect the cages and accessories before returning them to use. Please be aware that disinfection is not the same as cleaning! Cleaning removes dirt and debris through mechanical scrubbing and rinsing, but won't necessarily kill any pathogens that adhere to surfaces. Disinfection kills the germs, typically through heat or chemical processes. Many disinfectants don't work well in the presence of organic debris, so you will need to clean items thoroughly before you begin disinfecting. And, of course, never attempt to disinfect a cage

while your conure is in it, as it could be sickened by contact or overcome by fumes.

To disinfect, begin by choosing the proper product, and follow label instructions carefully! By their very nature, disinfectants are powerful chemicals designed to kill pathogens, so misuse can be very dangerous to your bird's health. Some commonly used brands are Wavicide, Nolvasan, Vanodine, Pet Focus, and Virkon. Ask your veterinarian for a recommendation of what's best for your situation if you're fighting a specific disease outbreak. Some pathogens are resistant to certain disinfectants, so one that works fine in some cases might not work well in others. It's important to know that all disinfectants have what is called a "contact time," which is the minimum time the product must stay in contact with the item to do its job. In most cases, it's a minimum of ten minutes. For disinfecting small items, soak them in a bucket or sink for the recommended time. For larger items such as cages, continually wipe or spray the surface to keep it wet with disinfectant for the recommended time. Once the disinfectant dries, it will not be completely effective.

Once the contact time has passed, rinse all items thoroughly and dry completely. Disinfectant residue can be irritating to skin, so be especially careful with perches or other items that your bird will be standing upon.

Always remember that most diseases are opportunistic, and will often attack a bird that is already weakened by poor housekeeping and stress. A happy pet in a clean and stress-free environment is likely to be a healthy pet that will share your life for many years to come.

PLAYTIME FOR YOUR CONURE

Play is an extremely important part of life for all animals, from birds to dogs to people, from young to old.

The Importance of Play

Humans tend to think of play as frivolous, something to be done when all the more pressing and important aspects of life are satisfied. That probably explains why so many people are tired, overwhelmed, and suffering from stress-related illnesses. Your conure knows better.

Play allows young animals and humans to practice social and survival skills, and helps to create new brain pathways in beings of all ages. Play stimulates the release of "feel-good" brain chemicals, and provides needed exercise to maintain health and fitness. Play is crucial to growth and development during youth, and helps ameliorate some of the ravages of age in the elderly.

Conures in general are playful birds, and a healthy, well-socialized conure will be looking for every opportunity possible to have fun. You can assist by providing a wide variety of safe and fun playthings, and by joining in interactive games with your pet. Playing together can cement your bond, and increase your bird's level of affection and trust toward humans.

Choosing Proper Toys

A proper toy needs to fulfill just a few criteria: it needs to be fun, safe, and interesting. It does not need to be expensive, or designed specifically for birds, or long lasting. In fact, some of my birds' favorite toys are simple household items that can be quickly destroyed and easily replaced. Years ago, I spent a small fortune on safe and indestructible bird toys, only to find that they sat in the cages

untouched. To a parrot, indestructible usually equates to boring. Conures love to chew, make noise, and disassemble their toys, so don't work to thwart those instincts. Instead, look for toys with lots of chewy wood or leather, knots to undo, parts that bang and clang, and brightly colored pieces. The trick is to provide safe fun. Here's where your common sense and attention to detail will come in handy.

I once received a panicky phone call from a new parrot owner who came home to find her bird happily chewing on small splinters of wood from a toy. She was convinced her bird would swallow the sharp bits of wood and die. I tried to reassure her, but instead she became incensed at my lack of concern. I finally asked, "What do you think they do in the wild?" Parrots, including conures, are cavity nesters.

That means they spend a great deal of their time excavating and chewing holes in trees to build their nests. It's very unlikely your bird will ever be harmed from chewing on safe substances such as wood, but it is important to supply wood that hasn't been chemically treated or exposed to pesticides.

Parrots are much like human toddlers, in that every item they find goes straight into their mouths. Your job is to provide them with nontoxic toys that aren't dangerous when chewed, and that don't create an entrapment hazard when your conure climbs and hangs from them. It's logical to think that toys manufactured specifically for pet birds will always be safe, but unfortunately that's not always the case. Always ask yourself a few questions before purchasing a bird toy:

1. Is this toy the appropriate size for my bird? A toy that is designed for smaller birds such as budgies or cockatiels might not be safe for a larger and stronger bird like your conure. Not only will it likely break quickly, but also it might contain tiny parts that your bird could accidentally swallow. A toy that's designed for much larger parrots probably won't pose any dangers, but could be intimidating to your pet. However, if your conure is bold and likes to explore, a large toy is just fine. Manufacturers usually group bird toys into small, medium, and large, but these are just guidelines. Your bird's personality will be the best guide.

2. Is this toy safe? This is sort of a trick question, because all toys can be dangerous under the wrong circumstances or with the wrong bird. There is always some risk in every item your bird comes into contact with, so safety is a relative concept. However, avoid toys with sharp edges, metal clasps or fasteners that can trap toes or beaks, and long loose strings that can pose a hanging hazard. In general, "S" hooks, key rings, and round jingle-type bells have proven to be dangerous, as are fabric or string toys in lengths that could ensnarl your bird. I've personally had to pry a crushed jingle bell off the beak of a very frightened bird that put the tip of her beak into the bell and bit down, effectively smashing it tightly around the sensitive beak tip. It was not a pleasant experience for either of us. Cowbell-type bells are considered safe, although if your conure can get its head inside, it will probably remove the clapper. Bird-safe tubular stainless steel bells are the best if you can find them. Key rings and "S" hooks are notorious for catching toes. Fasteners such as the C-shaped quick-links are usually safe, and are commonly used on bird toys.

Spend time monitoring your pet's play, and you'll soon learn what's okay and what's not.

3. Where was the toy manufactured? Some imported toys might be hidden sources of danger from lead-based paints or other unsafe materials. Try to stick with well-known manufacturers with experience in the pet bird market. Because excess zinc exposure is thought to contribute to a host of health issues, choose stainless steel fasteners and chains over zinc-plated nickel whenever possible.

4. Can this toy be cleaned, or is it inexpensive enough to replace when it gets dirty? Soft wood toys and most toys that include fabric or other porous materials can't really be cleaned effectively, so they should be considered disposable. All-fabric toys can sometimes be tossed in the laundry, but be very careful about how the dyes react with water. I once had a macaw that placed a dyed rope toy into his water dish, and then used it to "paint" the walls around his cage a somewhat shocking shade of electric blue. The food coloring-based dye was indeed safe for the bird, but unfortunately was not colorfast. It immediately bled out into the water, and I had to live with blue walls and a blue-legged macaw for many weeks until all traces of the dye finally scrubbed away. This toy passed the "fun, safe, and interesting" test with flying colors, but did not pass the "Oh-my-gosh-do-I want-this-in-my-house?" test. For a little more money, there are high quality stainless steel, acrylic, or nylon toys that are designed to last a long time, and these can often be run through the dishwasher or cleaned in hot soapy water as needed. Just make sure they're not boring!

Of course, you don't need to limit your choices to bird-specific toys. Some toys designed for dogs, cats, or even human babies make wonderful bird toys. Several of my birds absolutely love a popular human infant toy that plays classical music and flashes colored lights when a large button is pressed. It's intended as a hand toy for babies, but I use nylon ties to affix it to the cage bars and keep the rear battery compartment safely away from busy beaks. One of my birds plays with it so frequently that I've had to replace the batteries on a weekly basis.

Simple Toys

As mentioned before, toys don't need to be expensive to be fun. Simple household items can be used as toys. At Loro Parque, the world-renowned parrot park located in Tenerife in the Canary Islands, I once saw the staff handing out plastic drinking straws as a reward for the performing parrots. I tried this at home, and it was a huge hit. A package of brightly colored straws costs about a dollar, and your conure will enjoy chewing and tossing these colorful non-toxic treats. Unused straws from carryout restaurants are even more fun, because they come wrapped in paper that the bird can remove first.

Small paper or plastic cups can amuse a parrot for hours, although stay away from Styrofoam due to the possible dangers from ingestion. Empty tissue boxes and clean cardboard boxes are great fun for birds to tear up or use as secret hiding places. I've read of some concerns about the glue and other chemicals used in the manufacture of cardboard, but my parrots have been playing with cardboard for many years without any ill effects.

Again, the key is to use common sense. Don't ever allow your pet to chew on items that might have been contaminated with household chemicals, or that appear dirty, musty, or soiled. It's fine to let your conure chew up newspapers or plain junk mail, which is almost always printed with non-toxic inks. However, avoid glossy inks and papers, especially gift-wrapping papers. These might contain undesirable chemicals or heavy metals such as lead. I know it's cute to let your conure unwrap its own presents at the holidays, but stick to bird-safe wraps such as newsprint or brown paper bags.

Making Bird Toys

Another inexpensive option is to create your own bird toys. Craft stores, pet shops, and online bird stores are all great sources of toy parts. You can use sisal, rope, vegetable tanned leather, or smooth closed link chain as a base, and thread or tie goodies at various intervals. Some places sell pre-colored and drilled wood chunks, or you can make your own if you're handy with a drill. New Popsicle sticks or other pieces of craft wood in interesting shapes will be appealing chewies. To flavor and color the wood, mix some colored drink powder or flavored colored gelatin powder in a glass bowl with just enough water to cover the wood pieces, and soak until the wood reaches the desired color. Allow the pieces to dry thoroughly before adding to a toy. I usually bake them in a low oven—set at 150°F (65°C)—for about an hour to hasten the drying process. Tie on a bell or two, and you'll have a toy your conure will adore.

Besides wood shapes, feel free to experiment with other safe chewables. You can drill holes through cuttlebones or mineral blocks to sneak some healthy stuff into the toy, or string drilled nuts such as almonds and walnuts for a fun treat toy. Be creative and have fun!

Foot Toys

Conures love to roll around on their backs during play, and will enjoy a safe assortment of "foot toys." These are small, unattached toys that the bird can pick up and carry around, wrestle with, or pounce upon. Small wooden dumbbells, plastic Wiffle balls, and unbreakable rattles all make great foot toys. Some birds enjoy small stuffed toys, but these can't be cleaned easily and should be discarded when they become dirty or frayed.

You can also make toys from items at a hardware store. Conures are mechanical, and one of my birds' favorite simple toys is a long stainless steel bolt that I thread with stainless steel wing nuts. They love to unscrew the nuts, which I must then reattach. Some of my birds will attempt (usually unsuccessfully) to screw the nuts back on, and will play this game for hours. Always use stainless steel parts to avoid the unacceptable zinc levels in galvanized hardware.

Play Stands

Play stands come in many different styles, and can serve several important functions for your pet. The most basic is a simple T-shaped stand, which makes a great training aid because the bird can't easily turn a training session into a game of catch-me-if-you-can the way it could on a cage top. T-stands also provide a simple and economical way to move from room to room if you want to bring your conure with you around the house. Just be certain that the stand is sturdy enough to withstand being bumped without tipping over or flinging your bird to the floor. If you'll be keeping your conure on the stand for any length of time,

choose one that has detachable food and water cups, and possibly a tray to contain the mess.

For a more elaborate out-of-cage experience, the sky is the limit! Bird product manufacturers now market a wide array of play gyms and stands, designed for everything from tiny budgies to huge macaws. These play areas can help reduce boredom and territorial issues in parrots that might otherwise become cage-bound. You can use these as reward areas where your conure gets its favorite treat after a successful training session, or just as a place for your bird to blow off some steam after being caged all day. Just remember to supervise an uncaged bird at all times. It only takes a minute for a curious and mischievous conure to climb off its stand and get into trouble. Also, keep in mind that you'll need to maintain the play area, so look at possible choices with a critical eye for ease of cleaning.

Interactive Games

As mentioned at the beginning of this chapter, play will do both you and your pet a world of good. What could be better than playing together? Interactive play will stimulate your bird's mind and body, and strengthen your relationship. And, I think you'll find that those petty day-to-day worries we all face will fade quickly as you enjoy the clownish behavior of a tame and loving conure. Many of these games will be familiar, because you've probably played them with children. One caveat: games are only fun if both parties are having fun; be careful not to let any family members tease or torment your conure under the guise of "play."

Peekaboo

This classic baby game is usually a hit with parrots, and the variations are endless. You can be either the Boo-er or the Boo-ee. Hide behind a corner or a piece of furniture, and slowly peek out. When your conure notices you, shriek "peekaboo!" and duck back into hiding. Repeat. Eventually, your bird will probably begin to call for you when you're hiding, or will shriek excitedly when you pop out. To reverse the game, cover your pet's head with a paper towel or handkerchief. Pull it away quickly, act very surprised and say "peekaboo!" and immediately cover the bird again. It might take a few times until your conure gets the hang of the game, but once it does it will probably be a favorite. Don't be surprised if your bird learns the words and begins to initiate the game itself.

Find the Treat

This is a variation of the old magician's shell trick. Find a table or other flat surface where your bird can stand. You'll need three small paper cups and a special treat such as a sunflower seed, nut, or grape. Place the cups face down on the table. Engage the bird's attention, and slowly and obviously place the treat under one of the cups. Let him pick up the cup and retrieve the first treat. Now the game begins. Do it again, only this time move the cups around quickly and let your conure choose which cup is hiding the treat. Some parrots become amazingly adept at keeping their eyes on the treat cup, while others will simply charge forward and toss all the cups into the air. Either way, it's a lot of fun!

The Tickle Monster

This is a game that should be played only with conures that are already tame and trust-

ing. Don't attempt it if your pet is shy or fearful, as it might be genuinely frightened. If your bird enjoys lying on its back, flip it gently onto its back in the palm of your hand. Otherwise, allow it to stand on your open (face-up) palm. Stroke it gently for a moment, and then raise your hand up above its body. Wiggle your fingers, and say, "the tickle monster is coming!" Lower your fingers, quickly tickle the bird's belly or back, and raise your fingers again. Depending on your conure's tameness and enjoyment of the game, you can ramp up the suspense by raising your hand higher, making play growling sounds, and slowing down your descending hand until you "pounce." I have parrots that would play this for hours, squealing and kicking until they're exhausted. My Sun conure will solicit this game by rolling onto her back and saying, "tickle tickle!" Again, never force this game onto an unwilling bird, or you will terrify your pet and probably get bitten. Also, stop playing if you find your conure gets too wound up and begins to nip or act out. If that hap-

pens, I usually cuddle the bird against my chest and lower the energy.

Catch and Fetch

Dogs aren't the only pets that enjoy a good game of fetch. Be forewarned, when parrots play fetch, it is usually the human who does the fetching. For this game, find a small, lightweight plastic Wiffle-type ball with holes (some golf stores sell these as practice balls), or a small beanbag toy that your bird can grasp in its beak. Place your conure on a table or other flat surface, and gently toss or roll the toy so that it lands in front of the bird. Be extremely careful so that you don't hit the bird with the toy! I have seen parrots that actually learn to catch the toy as it's tossed. How the game proceeds is up to your pet. Some conures will try to bring or toss the toy back to you. Others will toss it onto the floor for you to retrieve. Still others will turn it into a rousing game of tug-of-war. Let your bird make up the rules, and don't forget to have fun!

UNDERSTANDING YOUR CONURE

Many bird books title this chapter "Taming and Training," but that implies that the conure does all the learning while the human teaches.

Ask anyone who's ever lived with a clever and manipulative conure, and you'll learn that it's often the other way around! A better approach is to look at things from your bird's point of view, and then work out a compromise you can both live with.

I can't stress this point enough: If you are looking for a pet that you can reliably dominate and control, then a parrot (especially a conure) is not the pet for you. Conures are smart, headstrong, and mischievous, and don't respond well to strict discipline or harsh training methods. If you're looking for an extremely intelligent and affectionate creature that usually will adapt to your wishes providing its own needs—both physical and emotional—are properly met, then you'll likely find a wonderful lifetime companion in a pet conure.

What to Expect from Your Conure

Because you are paying the rent or mortgage and providing the food, it's reasonable to expect that your wishes will trump those of your bird. Well, sort of. Your conure is certainly smart enough to figure out what you want, but keep in mind that you're dealing with a bundle of feathers with a high intellect and a low frustration level. That's where you need to be realistic in your expectations. It's okay to dig in your heels on the really important stuff, but don't try to win every battle or both you and the parrot will wind up frustrated, angry, and unhappy. Here's a rundown of what to expect.

✔ **Messiness:** Parrots are messy. You won't win this battle. In the wild, conures and other parrots help scatter plant seeds and reseed the environment through their wasteful and messy eating habits. They will do the same thing in your living room. It's an inherent part of their nature. Buy a hand vacuum, and hope that your dog enjoys scavenging on leftover fruit and seeds.

✔ **Screaming:** Parrots are loud, and some conures take this trait to new heights. *Aratinga* and *Nandayus* species are especially infamous for their frequent and loud vocalizations. Wild conures use vocalizations to remain in contact with their flock mates, warn of predators, and advise the flock of newfound food sources. Although you'll never be able to quell this trait entirely (nor should you attempt to), it is reasonable to expect your pet to play quietly at times, and not to simply scream mindlessly from dawn to dusk. We'll discuss behavioral problem solving later in this chapter.

✔ **Biting:** Parrots bite for a variety of reasons, mostly due to fear or aggression. If your bird is biting out of fear, it's up to you to figure out and remove the perceived threat. If your conure bites out of aggression, here's where you should dig in your heels. Conures can be bossy, but they must be taught that biting and bullying are unacceptable behaviors. However, never strike a bird or react in violence, or your relationship can be forever damaged once trust is destroyed. Besides, aggressive behavior on your part will only create more fear and/or aggression in your bird, thereby escalating the unwanted behavior.

✔ **Chewing and destruction:** Parrots chew. As discussed earlier in the book, they are cavity nesters and their ability to reproduce in the wild depends on their ability to hollow out a suitable nesting cavity. You won't exactly win this battle, but you can claim victory through trickery and subterfuge; that is, give them something acceptable to chew on in lieu of your new dining room set. And always supervise out of cage time. A bored conure doesn't understand that electric cords and wall moldings weren't designed to be beak toys.

What Your Conure Expects from You

Humans are often amazingly self-absorbed when it comes to animals. It never occurs to some people that our pets have valid expectations from us, and if we are unable or unwilling to meet these expectations we probably shouldn't keep a companion animal in the first place. Conures are not low-maintenance pets. Your bird will have needs and wants that go beyond the basics needed for survival. Consider the following.

✔ **Food, water, and shelter:** These basics are obviously required, but the quality you provide can spell the difference between surviving and thriving. Spend the money on a great cage and excellent food. If you can't afford it, perhaps you should consider a cheaper and lower-maintenance pet.

✔ **Veterinary care:** Medical care is non-negotiable. If your conure requires veterinary assistance, you must provide it. You have voluntarily accepted responsibility for the bird, so please do the right thing. If a medical emergency arises and you're financially strained (as many folks are these days) discuss payment options with your vet. Some animal clinics will accept payment plans, or can direct you to someone who will.

✔ **Love and attention:** These are also non-negotiable. Conures are highly social flock ani-

mals. In the wild, being ostracized from the flock means almost certain death from predators or starvation. Wild parrots are rarely singular; nearly every moment of their day is filled with cooperative activities within a flock or within a monogamous bond. They typically mate for life, and are capable of deep love and abundant affection. An ignored or neglected parrot will be absolutely miserable and prone to serious behavioral disorders as it attempts to cope with its circumstances. Please don't consider a pet conure unless you have the ability to spend quality time with it on a daily basis. Of course, a well-loved and healthy conure will cut its owner an occasional break for vacations or extra-busy temporary work schedules, but long stretches of inattention can cause

the bird to act out in negative ways through screaming, biting, or feather plucking.

✔ **Structure and discipline:** In light of what I've said so far, this might come as a surprise, but yes, your conure will be looking to you to "lead the flock." Wild parrots live according to the sun and to the seasons. Their survival depends in large part on their ability to adapt to and predict what their environment will provide. Rainy seasons bring food and water, enough to allow parent birds to settle down and rear chicks. Droughts mean hunger and thirst, and the need to range farther to search for sustenance. In captivity, your conure will quickly learn, for example, that the sound of your alarm clock coincides with the sunrise, and means fresh food is on the way. If the alarm doesn't sound on the weekend, your conure might start yelling the parrot equivalent of "Hey, what's going on?" shortly after sunrise. You certainly don't need to run your life with military precision, but some semblance of structure, especially established wake-up and bedtimes for the bird, will give it a sense of security.

✔ **Consistency and trust:** This is similar to structure, but more personal. Your conure has the capacity to bond deeply with you and other family members, provided it knows that you can be trusted. If you're moody and unpredictable, petting the bird one moment and screaming at it the next, that trust will never develop. Please don't use your conure as a scapegoat for other problems in your life. Always treat the bird with kindness and respect, and you'll find it returned tenfold.

Working with Your Conure

Before you begin the process of teaching your conure how your household "flock" operates, I suggest you take your pet to a veterinarian or groomer for a proper wing clip. The photo below left displays a wing clip, but it is important to observe the procedure at least once before attempting it yourself. Wing clips are temporary and painless, much like a human haircut. The purpose isn't to cause the bird to drop like a rock if it attempts to fly, but instead to prevent it from gaining altitude or speed.

Wing Clipping vs. Free Flight

Some folks feel that it's cruel to clip a bird's wings, and argue that parrots were intended to fly. The problem is that parrots weren't really intended to live in captivity either, along with the attendant hazards and constraints. And, although conures have the proven ability to thrive in captivity, loss of free flight is often one of the trade-offs. A free-flighted bird is at extreme risk for escape and injury (flying into mirrors, windows, and ceiling fans, to name a few), and it will possibly develop behavioral issues from the unrestricted freedom. After all, how likely would it be that a toddler would behave if he or she could simply fly to the top of the bookcase to avoid mom and dad's discipline? You're dealing with a feathered toddler, and one that is perfectly capable of climbing and walking from one place to the next.

Feathers do grow out; once you and your conure are totally comfortable with each other, and you're reasonably comfortable with its willingness to obey, you can always let its feathers grow and experiment with free flight. There certainly are some benefits—it's great exercise, and will improve a bird's coordination—but as mentioned, it is somewhat fraught with danger. For a new bird, especially a first bird, I always recommend wing clips.

Height and Dominance

There's a cherished belief in parrot psychology that height equals dominance. It makes sense, because the dominant or "alpha" bird in a flock gets first choice of prime real estate, which is almost always the highest perch. I don't believe it's the actual height per se, but instead the control of height that matters. In other words, if the alpha parrot suddenly decided that the lowest perch, or the one closest to the water source, or the one most protected from the wind was most desirable, he would boot off the lower-ranking bird and take that spot. Therefore, if you are to play the role of alpha parrot, you must control your bird's access to perching.

The easiest way to do this is through height control. In general, don't let your pet play on surfaces that are above human eye level. For the same reasons, don't allow your conure to ride around on top of your head. One of the quickest ways to perform an attitude adjustment on a persnickety parrot is to momentarily place it on the floor. Most (but not all) parrots feel vulnerable on the floor, and will quickly decide to behave if you will pick them up.

Step Up Command

The "step up" command is one of the most important commands you will ever teach your bird. This command allows you to move the bird from place to place, retrieve it from danger, and correct misbehavior. To begin, place the conure on a training stand or the back of a chair. Place your index finger (or the side of your hand for larger, heavier conures) against the bird's abdomen, press lightly, and say, "step up." If it obeys and steps onto your hand, praise it lavishly, then return it to the perch and repeat. You can also use the command "down" or "off" as you encourage it to step off your hand. Don't use "step down" because the bird might only hear the first word and become confused. Again, give lots of praise when it obeys.

If the conure refuses to step up, ducks sideway, or runs away, reevaluate your technique. Make sure the chair or stand is suitable to limit the bird's mobility—don't use complex play stands or large overstuffed chairs that allow your pet room to escape rather than obey. A plain wooden straight-backed chair or simple T-stand is best. Make your movements fluid and rapid, and give the command simultaneously. The trick is to offer the command with authority, and move your hand against the bird quickly and with enough gentle pressure that it has no choice but to step up or lose its balance. Don't give it time to consider its other options, such as biting or running away.

On the other hand, don't ever force the bird off balance so much that it falls off the perch. Also, make sure you position your hand low enough so that your pet can step up with ease. I often see new owners place their hands high against their birds' chests. When the conure attempts to clamber up by grabbing the finger with its beak, the person yanks his or her hand away, thinking that the bird is attempting to bite; the bird falls, and both owner and parrot are suspicious and frustrated.

Once your pet has the hang of this command, you can reinforce and practice by playing the "ladder game." Hold the conure on one index finger, and then offer your other index finger while saying "step up." Continue in this manner, simulating the action of your bird climbing a ladder. This is good exercise, and your conure will think it's a fun game. Don't be surprised if your pet begins to use the command to ask to be picked up. Many of my parrots will lift a foot and ask, "step up?" when they want some affection.

Speech Training

All conures can learn to mimic human speech, but not all do. Please don't ever buy a parrot just for the novelty of speech. You can't force a disinterested bird to talk, and your love shouldn't be contingent upon the conure's ability to amuse your friends. Most pet conures will likely learn at least a few words, especially those that they hear frequently or that are said with emotion. Keep that in mind when you're tempted to scream "shut up" at a noisy bird; it's likely you'll soon hear your own unpleasant words shouted back at you.

In general, parrots repeat words they find interesting. Higher-pitched voices such as those from women and children often catch their interest faster than deeper or monotone voices. If you want to teach your pet to talk, repeat simple words or phrases with emotion and excitement. Don't be discouraged if it seems like nothing is happening at first. Parrots seem to process human speech internally for quite a while before they begin to mimic. I've noticed that they often begin by counting out syllables. In other words, if you're teaching "pretty bird," (three syllables), your conure might begin by grunting or squeaking three times in the same cadence. They will

next fill in sounds they already know, until they finally put together the entire word or phrase.

The good news is that once they finally master their first words, new words come more quickly. I have an extremely articulate African grey parrot that can now repeat words after hearing them just once or twice, even though it took her close to six months to learn her first word. You might be surprised to hear your pet mumbling quietly to itself in the dark after you've put it to bed. For some reason, many parrots seem to love to practice speech as they're nodding off to sleep.

Some things I don't recommend are the CD or tape programs that promise to teach your bird to talk. These programs might teach your bird to mindlessly mimic sound patterns, but it will have no idea what it is saying or why. I'm a strong believer that parrots are capable of at least limited cognitive speech. In other words, they can learn to assign meaning to the words they say and use them appropriately. If, for example, you say "apple" every time you offer your conure a slice of apple, it will soon associate that word with the fruit, and may use it to request that treat. Scientists call this "labeling," and are very careful to distinguish it from true cognitive speech. However, these scientists haven't lived with my African grey, and have never seen how she orders everyone in the household to fulfill her every whim in clear and concise English. Labeling, indeed!

Trick Training

Clever conures are also capable of learning simple tricks. There are some excellent books and props on the market that can help you turn your pet into a circus star, but there are also a few simple tricks you can teach by simply taking advantage of your bird's natural tendencies. Keep in mind that trick training should be fun, so never stress or overwork your pet in the process.

Parrots learn tricks through a process known as "operant conditioning." What this means is that the bird learns that by performing a certain prescribed action (the "operant response"), it will get a treat. I don't believe in using treats (other than praise) for teaching good behavior—that's like bribing kids to obey—but trick training is a little different. Because a trick is a specific behavior that serves no real purpose other than amusement, and because it needs to be performed on command, I think food rewards help to reinforce the action and entice the bird to perform. For the same reasons, never discipline your pet or show disapproval if it refuses to perform the trick. Just move on and try again later.

To begin trick training, make sure your pet is alert and calm. Don't grab a sleepy, cranky, or overly hungry conure and expect it to perform. Trick training consists of four basic parts: the "cue" or command, the action, the "bridge," and the reward. The bridge is a noise or a signal that lets the bird know it has acted properly, and will be rewarded—much like the bells and whistles that go off when a game show contestant answers correctly. Many dog trainers (and some bird trainers) use hand-held clickers as a bridge when the animal performs on cue. A bridge sort of freezes the moment (and the specific action) in time so that the bird knows exactly what it did to earn the reward. A quick and enthusiastic "good bird!" works well as a bridge, followed immediately by a reward such as a single hulled sunflower seed, piece of nut, or small bite of apple. The reward should be very tiny, but very

tasty. You want the bird to continue to work, not stuff down a large treat and want a nap. For extra emphasis, use the cue word in the bridge, such as "Good play dead!" or "Good dance!"

The key to training is patience and more patience. The first trick, like the first word, might be seemingly forever in coming. Once it dawns on your pet that you are simply asking it to mimic a behavior, and that it will be consistently rewarded for doing so, it will likely learn subsequent tricks at a much faster rate. Remember to quit whenever the bird seems

tired or bored, but try to end the session on a positive note after a successful attempt at the desired action. The following are some simple tricks that build on a conure's natural behavior. These are very brief descriptions, and you might need to reference a more in-depth training guide or seek out a trainer for more assistance.

✔ **Play dead.** Tame conures usually are more than willing to lie on their backs, and this is the basis for the trick. Begin by accustoming your pet to lie quietly on its back in your hand. At this point, don't cue the bird, just gently stroke it and calm it. Once you feel it is relaxed and receptive, take your finger and very gently push its head back against your hand, while giving the command "play dead." Immediately bridge and reward. At this point, the bird hasn't really done anything, and it will probably be thinking "Huh?" Repeat, but each time wait a tiny bit

longer to bridge. If your bird lifts its head or stands up, don't bridge or reward any more that session unless it remains "dead" for at least a couple seconds. Eventually (and it might take many sessions) the conure will understand the trick. Once it does, you can begin expanding the trick by giving the cue while the bird is standing, and teaching it to lie down, roll over, and play dead from the original cue. Please note that the cue can be any words you choose, but always be completely consistent—even the tiniest change of words might confuse the bird and cause a major setback. A friend of mine once taught his Senegal parrot to play dead using the cue word "bang" combined with the visual cue of pointing a finger gun-style. Needless to say, it was an adorable trick that got a lot of attention, and the bird started to perform on its own, saying "bang" and then falling over.

✔ **Dance.** Conures are active parrots that naturally sway and pace when excited. Put on some upbeat music, and begin to dance around in front of your bird. Cue "dance!" If your conure sways or bobs its head in response, bridge "good dance!" and reward. Soon you'll have a dancin' fool on your hands.

✔ **Shake hands.** Once your conure has learned the important behavioral "step up" command, it will likely begin to lift its foot in anticipation as your hand moves near. To teach this trick, gently grasp the foot and shake it while cueing "shake hands." Bridge and reward. If the bird doesn't automatically lift its foot, gently lift and shake the foot while cueing. To avoid confusion, make sure to give clear commands so that the bird knows what you want it to do: step up, or shake hands? Once the conure clearly understands the trick, you can refine it by delaying the bridge/reward until it actually places its foot into your outstretched fingers.

✔ **Eagle.** If your conure is tame and enjoys being handled, "eagle" is a simple trick to learn. I teach this trick by first demonstrating, just like dance. I spread out my arms and lower my head in my best approximation of an eagle's pose, while saying "eagle!" Next I gently spread out my bird's wings on cue, then bridge and reward. A full-wing stretch feels good, so it's sort of a self-rewarding action anyway. The trick is to teach the bird to respond on cue, and hold the pose a few seconds or longer.

Problem Behaviors

What if the trick's on you, and your conure turns into a feathered demon? Behavioral problems such as screaming and biting can strain your relationship with your bird at best, and have caused many pet birds to be dumped into shelters or worse.

To begin, always have your pet thoroughly examined by a veterinarian to rule out any physical causes, especially if the unwanted behaviors appeared suddenly. Hidden injuries or illness can cause pain and irritability that your pet has no way of expressing except through acting out. If health issues are at the root, your bird will probably return to its old sweet self after appropriate treatment. Once it gets a clean bill of health, it's time to look at psychological issues.

Parrots don't do anything unless they have a reason: the behavior must serve some purpose, or it won't often be repeated. Now, the reason might not be apparent to you, or might not make sense to a human, but trust that it is a valid reason in your bird's mind. Your job as a "parrot parent" is to sleuth out the reason and provide the proper antidote. For example, if your conure screams because it's hungry, solve the problem by rearranging the feeding schedule or amount of food so that hunger is never an issue. Of course, few behavioral problems are so obvious or easily solved, but the point is that you must look beyond the behavior to get at the underlying cause.

Screaming

As mentioned earlier, conures are vocal birds by nature, and some screaming is normal and expected, especially for brief periods in the morning and evening, or when family members first arrive home. If, however, your pet screams from dawn to dusk, or screeches hysterically every time you leave the room, with enough volume to cause your brain to bleed, that's problem screaming.

Parrots scream for many reasons: to stay in contact with their flock, to warn others of dan-

ger, or to express fear or anger. Captive parrots can also begin to scream from sheer boredom. Look at the world from your conure's eyes. Is there a soaring hawk or stalking cat in view from the window? Is the bird lonely or bored, calling to its human flock? Is there a family argument going on that is distressing the bird? Or a loud or scary television program? If you can pinpoint when the bird is most likely to scream, you'll be close to discovering why. Parrots react much more strongly to visual cues than they do to sound, so pulling the shade or covering the bird's cage until the "danger" passes should quell fear-based screaming.

For boredom and loneliness, the best antidote is to allow the conure to come out and participate in family activities. Of course, that's not always feasible, and your pet does need to learn to amuse itself at times. Make sure it has an interesting array of toys, and, if possible, position the cage so that the bird can at least see

its humans. If it continues to call and screech, speak softly to reassure it that you're nearby, but don't jump up and run to the cage to either correct or comfort it. If you do, you've just taught the bird that screaming works! After all, mom and dad came running just as it had hoped they would. Your conure won't care that you're red-faced and angry; it will just be pleased that you responded to its call.

If the screaming still persists, it's okay to cover the bird's cage for a brief time-out. Here's where many parrot owners make a serious mistake. They cover the cage, the bird stops screaming, and they don't return to uncover it, because all is quiet. Eventually, the bird gets bored and lonely, and begins to scream again, despite the cover. The key is to return to the cage as soon as the bird remains quiet for a few minutes, uncover it, and praise lavishly. Once you repeat this process a few times (more likely a few dozen times) or more, your conure will eventually learn it is ostracized from the flock for excessive screaming, but rewarded for quiet behavior. Please note that bad habits take time, patience, and consistency to break, but they will disappear eventually if they're not inadvertently enforced.

Biting

Biting is a habit that can be heartbreaking to owners who think it means that their beloved pet doesn't love them back. Parrots don't think that way, so try not to take it personally. Aggressive biting is usually just your conure's way of trying to train or bully you into following its whims and wishes. It might be attempting to usurp your position as alpha bird. It might be trying to chase you to safety in order to protect you from perceived danger. (Remember that circling hawk?) It might be displaced aggression, and it's biting you because it can't get to the dog that really ticked it off this afternoon. There's an old saying that parrots live by the motto "if you can't bite the one you want, bite the one you're with."

Correcting problem biting is much like correcting problem screaming. Begin by analyzing when and where your bird bites. If you can decipher a pattern, you might be able to simply remove the trigger. If it seems to be just generalized bullying, there are a few steps you can take to reduce the problem.

1. Be aware of your conure's body language. Excited or angry parrots can rapidly constrict and dilate the pupils of their eyes, a behavior referred to as "flashing" or "pinning" their eyes. Ruffled nape feathers, an open beak, and flashing eyes are all likely signs of an impending bite. Don't reach for a parrot displaying this posture, or you will get bitten.

2. Execute the step up command. If your bird reaches down to bite instead of stepping up, say "No!" loudly and sharply, and snap the fingers of your other hand to distract the bird as you complete the maneuver. Don't yank your hand back, or you will quickly lose control of the command, and it will degenerate into a game of dodge and bite for your conure.

3. If the bird attempts to bite while it is standing on your hand, give it what parrot behaviorist Chris Davis refers to as an "earthquake." Rapidly tilt or drop your hand a few inches to throw the bird slightly off balance. It can't bite and regain its balance at the same time, and it will quickly learn that biting hands causes earthquakes. Of course, never drop the bird to the ground or it might be injured.

If these quick tips don't work, your veterinarian can probably recommend a parrot behaviorist who can work with you either over the telephone or in person. Just remember that your conure has a reason to act the way it does. A smart owner will help the bird find reasons to act in a more civilized and acceptable manner.

HEALTHY NUTRITION

A healthy diet is the basis for a long and vital life, but don't forget that food should be pleasurable as well, perhaps even fun!

It's not always easy to strike a balance between good taste and proper nutrition—as anyone who has ever been on a diet can testify—but your conure's health and happiness depends on your ability to feed it properly. If you don't choose wisely, your pet will suffer.

One problem with poor food choices is that the effect is often slow and insidious. Malnutrition does kill, but usually under the guise of chronic disease. It's easy to miss the link between the high-fat seed diet eaten by a pet bird, and its eventual death from cardiovascular disease at age ten. When you look at the larger picture and realize that other conures of the same species frequently live into their twenties or thirties, only then does it become obvious that something went wrong. Of course, by then it's too late.

You can't trust your conure to make the right choices either when it has the opportunity to eat birdie junk food. It hasn't read the latest nutritional studies, and will eat what tastes best, or what is most familiar. Would you choose broccoli over ice cream if weight and health issues didn't exist in your mind?

In the wild, conures are opportunistic feeders that eat whatever they can to sustain life: plants, insects, seeds, fruits, flowers, nuts, and perhaps even small lizards. That doesn't mean we should attempt to duplicate a free-ranging bird's diet. Wild conures rarely attain a maximum life expectancy, due in part to the difficulty of obtaining sufficient and nutritious food. So what should they eat—or not eat—in captivity?

Seed Diets

Up until the early 1990s, the basic diet for pet birds was a seed mix. We now know that seeds alone are woefully inadequate for most parrots, especially conures, which seem to have

an even higher need for certain nutrients than some other parrots. For example, *hypocalcemia,* a metabolic calcium deficiency, can trigger conure bleeding syndrome, a chronic and eventually fatal blood disorder that affects some conures. (See the following chapter for more information on this disease.) Conures are also prone to vitamin A deficiencies, which can lead to a host of problems, including sinus and respiratory issues and skin disorders. Seed mixes are lacking in vitamins A, D_3, E, K, most B vitamins, calcium and several other minerals, and some amino acids. In short, seeds provide precious few nutrients yet are high in fat. Unfortunately,

seeds (especially sunflower) taste really good, and given the choice, most parrots would happily eat a diet of pure seeds. The result is a parrot that is obese yet malnourished at the same time. Seeds are great as a carefully limited treat offered in small amounts—about a teaspoon a day—but should never make up the bulk of your bird's daily diet. And don't be fooled into thinking that a "fortified" seed diet will be much better; most manufacturers accomplish this by adding some fortified pellets. If your conure tosses those pellets onto the floor for the dog or shoves them aside in its quest for sunflower, it will not be gaining any additional nutrition.

Nutrient Functions and Sources

Selected Nutrient	What It Does	Good Sources
Vitamin A	Protects skin and mucous membranes; promotes eye health; enhances immunity.	Carrots, squash, sweet potatoes, kale, cantaloupe, peaches, papaya, mango, apricots.
Vitamin C	Promotes collagen formation; enhances calcium and iron absorption; builds strong bones and blood vessels; aids in wound healing.	Red berries, kiwi, oranges, broccoli, bell peppers, spinach. Note that some bird species metabolize vitamin C in the liver, but dietary sources are still important.
Vitamin D_3	Required for calcium and phosphorus metabolism; builds bones; aids cellular energy functions.	Fish oil, egg yolks, fortified foods. Note that vitamin D is metabolized from sunlight, but indoor birds require dietary sources.
Vitamin E	Potent antioxidant; protects cells from damage; aids fertility; maintains health of red blood cells; aids immune function.	Nuts, seeds, whole grains, wheat germ, asparagus, egg yolks.
Vitamin K	Required for proper blood clotting; works with vitamin D_3 in calcium metabolism; aids in cellular energy metabolism.	Broccoli, kale, spinach, Swiss chard, parsley, turnip greens. Note that vitamin K is synthesized by bacteria in the lower intestine, but absorption can be disrupted for many reasons.
B-Complex Vitamins	Water-soluble vitamins with wide-ranging effects; critical for energy production, cell metabolism, and nervous system functions; required for health of skin, eyes, feathers, brain, and digestive tract.	Whole grains, molasses, brewer's yeast, nuts, green leafy vegetables, yogurt.
Calcium	Builds bones; critical for proper function of nerves and muscles, including heart; aids in blood health and clotting; deficiency can trigger conure bleeding syndrome in susceptible birds.	Calcium blocks and cuttlebone, cheese, yogurt, Brazil nuts, broccoli, collard greens, kale, mustard greens, bok choy.

Formulated Diets

Our current knowledge of parrot nutritional needs has led pet food scientists to create formulated diets for pet birds. Based on the extruded or pelleted diets designed for dogs, cats, and rabbits, these foods are an easy way to combat the chronic malnutrition that has plagued captive birds in the past. Although extruded foods and pelleted foods are manufactured through different processes, they both combine high quality grains, vitamins, minerals, and other ingredients into a dough or mash that is then formed into bird-sized morsels. They're often flavored and colored (sometimes naturally, sometimes not) to entice finicky eaters. A majority of the brands on the market today are extruded, but most bird people tend to use the term "pellets" as a catch-all phrase to describe any formulated diet. These diets provide excellent nutrition and prevent selective food choices. You can find one your conure likes and stick with it, or switch off between brands to prevent boredom. Either way, a formulated diet should make up about 60 to 80 percent of your conure's complete diet.

Grains, Beans, and Nuts

Human food manufacturers are finally catching on to what aviculturists have known for a long time: Whole grains are chock full of health benefits, and taste great as well. Cooked grains, such as brown rice, whole-wheat pasta, and unsweetened oatmeal can serve as a delicious comfort-food meal for your conure. Although most whole grains are packed with nutrients and are low in fat, they are missing a few essential amino acids, so they don't supply a "complete" protein. That's where beans (legumes) come in! Beans are also healthy and most are low in fat, and supply the amino acids missing from grains. Together, these complementary foods supply a wonderful source of complete protein, in addition to all their other nutrients. Humans do this food-combining all the time without giving it much thought: rice and beans, and peanut butter sandwiches are two examples. Peanut butter sandwiches? Yes, peanuts are actually legumes, not nuts, and combined with whole grain bread provide a protein punch along with vitamins, minerals, and heart-healthy fats. Your conure will love to share a tiny bit of your sandwich, but avoid highly sweetened peanut butters and refined breads. Nuts of all types are healthy treats, provided they're unsalted. They are high in fat, but it's mostly the heart-healthy kind. Just limit quantities if your conure needs to be watching its weight.

Fruits and Veggies

A wide array of colorful fruits and vegetables will add flavor, texture, and enhanced nutrition to your conure's menu. Wild conures, especially the *Pyrrhura spp.*, eat a lot of fruit, and your domestic pet will enjoy it too. You can feed your conure almost any fruit or vegetable, with the exception of avocado, raw onions, and rhubarb. For reasons that are poorly understood, avocado has proven to be fatal to some birds, so don't let your pet dip into the guacamole. Scattered reports of rhubarb toxicity exist, and raw onions are a possible source of

Canary-winged parakeets (**Brotogeris versicolurus**) *are occasionally placed under the conure umbrella by scientists, but are not considered conures in aviculture.*

Pseudomonas bacteria and other toxins. And, if you have other pets, be careful about allowing your conure to share its treats with them. Grapes and raisins, for example, are healthy and often-coveted parrot treats, but are toxic to dogs and possibly cats. So are onions in any form. Conures frequently enjoy tossing food to dogs, but keep an eye on what they toss.

When choosing fruits and veggies for your bird, always aim for the freshest produce available (organic if possible), and wash it thoroughly. Frozen thawed veggies are fine, but avoid canned due to the usual high sodium content. If you must use canned, choose low-sodium versions and rinse to remove some of the sodium before feeding. (See chart for selected nutrients and their sources.) This is by no means a complete listing, but it will help you understand the importance of a varied diet.

People Foods

Conures' nutritional requirements are surprising similar to humans, so go ahead and share your meals with your bird. That is, share your healthy meals—your conure should avoid salty, fried, high-fat, highly refined, and sugar-laden foods. Some treats, such as pasta and pizza, are

*Barred (or Lineolated) parakeets (**Bolborhynchus lineola**) are another species that some ornithologists place with conures. Like the **Brotogeris spp.**, these are not considered conures by the avicultural world.*

very attractive to parrots, and you might find that your feathered buddy won't let you indulge without sharing. Don't ever share your vices, however; nicotine, alcohol, chocolate, and caffeine are all poisonous to birds, so keep the Ben & Jerry's and Starbucks to yourself. Also be aware that conures are missing lactase, the digestive enzyme needed to digest lactose, the natural sugar in milk products. They can handle small bits of cheese and yogurt, which provide a great source of calcium, because processing and fermentation of these products reduces the lactose content considerably. Just don't overdo it, or your conure could suffer serious indigestion and intestinal upset.

Water

Water isn't often thought of as a nutrient, but in fact it's one of the most important nutrients of all. Be certain that your conure has a supply of fresh, clean water available at all times. Dehydration strikes quickly, and dirty water can create a dangerous bacterial soup. Most conures love to play in the water, and will drop food, toys, discarded feathers, and poop into the water dish over the course of a day. Always clean and refill the dish at least once a day, more often in warm weather or when your bird has been playing in it.

If your water comes from a municipal source, it's probably fine straight from the tap. If you have well water, be sure to test as recommended to insure the safety and health of your conure and your family. If in doubt, consult with a professional about a water filtration system that will best remove the contaminants in your water supply. Bottled water is also an option, but be aware that many brands of bottled water are simply taken from municipal sources, and often aren't any purer or healthier than what comes from your tap.

The healthiest diets are those that include a wide array of fresh foods. Cooking for your conure is a fun way to provide good nutrition and tempting tastes. Try some of the recipes below, or experiment with making some of your old family favorites bird-friendly. You just might be tempted to double the recipes and enjoy some yourself!

Conure Corn Cupcakes

1¾ cups stone ground
  cornmeal
¾ cup whole-wheat flour
3 teaspoons baking powder
1 teaspoon baking soda
½ teaspoon salt
1½ cups soymilk (you can substitute rice milk, almond
  milk, or buttermilk if desired)
3 large eggs
3 tablespoons applesauce

2 tablespoons honey or agave
  nectar for sweetness if
  desired.
  Optional: Add up to two
cups chopped nuts, chopped
or dried fruits, chopped veggies, calcium powder, chili
peppers, or any healthy ingredients you choose.

  Combine the meal, flour,
baking powder, soda, and salt in
a large mixing bowl. In another
bowl, whisk together the eggs,
soymilk, and applesauce. Pour
the soymilk mixture into the
dry mixture and stir until all
ingredients are moistened. Stir
in any optional ingredients. Fill
greased mini muffin cups about
¾ full. Bake at 425°F (218°C)
for 15 to 20 minutes, or until
browned and firm to a light
touch. Makes about 24 to 36
cupcakes, depending on
amount of optional ingredients

added. These freeze well for
future use.

Crazy Conure Confetti Salad

Approximately ½ apple, diced
Approximately ½ raw or
  baked sweet potato, diced
1 cup prepackaged cole slaw
  mix with shredded carrots,
  shredded red cabbage, or
  broccoli slaw
1 handful mixed greens, torn
  into tiny pieces
Several grapes, halved or
  quartered
1 tablespoon shelled chopped
  nuts: walnuts, pecans,
  almonds, or Brazil nuts.
  Toss all ingredients well,
and refrigerate for up to three
days.

Sweet Potato Surprise

  Bake or microwave one
small sweet potato until soft.
Cut in half and scoop the flesh
into a small bowl, retaining
the skin. Add golden raisins,
chopped nuts, and drained
crushed pineapple or dried
pineapple bits. Sprinkle with
a small amount of honey, or
preferably molasses if you
have it. Mash together well,
divide, and scoop mixture back
into potato skin halves. Cut
the halves again so that you
now have four servings. These
can be frozen for future use.

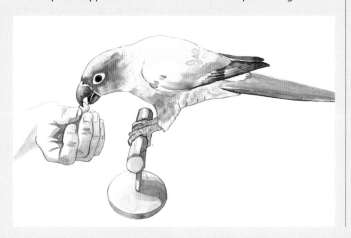

CONURES

South Of The Border Salad

1 cup frozen or fresh corn
1 cup canned black beans, rinsed well
½ green or red bell pepper, diced
1 jalapeno pepper, seeded and diced
¼ cup of fresh cilantro leaves
Dressing:
1 teaspoon extra virgin olive oil
2 teaspoons rice wine vinegar or apple cider
   vinegar
1 teaspoon lime juice

Whisk olive oil, vinegar, and lime juice to combine. Mix corn, beans, and peppers in a bowl, sprinkle with dressing and toss to coat. Add cilantro leaves and serve.

Spinach, Egg, and Cheese Scramble

Spray a small frying pan (no Teflon, please!) with non-stick cooking spray. Scramble together one egg, a small handful of torn or chopped spinach leaves, and about a teaspoon of crumbled feta cheese. Cook until firm. Let cool slightly before serving.

Multigrain Madness

1 cup long grain brown rice
1 cup millet
1 cup of whole barley
1 cup of whole oats (groats)
½ cup of wild rice, or a mixture of wild type
   rices
1 teaspoon salt
1 or 2 cans of cooked beans, any variety.
   (I prefer black or red for their high nutritional value.)
½ cup chopped walnuts

Mix together rices, millet, barley, and oats. Rinse well to remove dust and debris, and then place in a heavy pot. Cover with enough water to sit about 2 inches (5 cm) deep over the top of the grains. Add salt and stir. Bring to a boil, stir, and reduce heat to a low simmer. Cook until grains are tender and water is reduced, about 35 minutes. Add rinsed beans and walnuts, and mix well. Depending on your conure's tastes, you can add savory spices such as cumin, chili powder, oregano, or crushed red peppers, or sweet spices such as cinnamon or pumpkin pie spice. I freeze this mixture in ice cube trays, and simply pop out a cube and microwave when I want a quick hearty dinner for my birds. One caution: Be extremely careful when microwaving food for your conure! Stir and test thoroughly to avoid burning your pet from hotspots in the food.

As you can see, cooking for conures is fun, and not that different from cooking for the rest of your family. Just focus on healthy ingredients, pay attention to the tastes and textures that capture your bird's interest, and soon you'll have a feathered gourmand on your hands.

YOUR CONURE IN HEALTH AND DISEASE

Many bird diseases are opportunistic and predatory. They don't often attack individuals that are happy, well fed, and living in a clean environment.

Usually, the best prevention for illness is maintaining a focus on daily wellness, which, just like in humans, means diet, exercise, and stress management.

Now, it's not really necessary to enroll your conure in a yoga class, but be aware of common physical stressors that we've discussed in other sections of this book, such as insufficient lighting, poor air quality, a dirty cage, and bad dietary choices. And don't discount the power of love. A well-loved pet that receives plenty of affection is more likely to stay healthy than a physically sound but emotionally bereft bird.

Unfortunately, diseases do occasionally strike despite our best care. When that happens, early detection and prompt treatment will give your conure its best chance for survival. If you ever notice your pet displaying any of the symptoms of illness described in the second chapter of this book, contact your veterinarian immediately. Sometimes it's just a subtle change in the bird's behavior, but trust your instincts. A veterinarian friend of mine lists this hard to define symptom as "ADR"—"ain't doin' right"—and considers it an important indicator of illness. The point is that you are probably the only one who will pick up on the first tiny clues: frequent lethargy in a usually bouncy bird, reduced vocalizing in a chatty conure, or maybe just uncharacteristic disinterest in family pizza night. When you hear that nagging voice in the back of your head, it's time to schedule a visit to the vet for a checkup.

Common Diseases

Many of the problems that affected wild-caught and imported birds of years past rarely exist in domestically bred conures. For example, worms and other parasites were a common issue with imports, but conures raised and kept indoors won't be exposed and should never become infected. If you do house your conures outdoors, there are parasites and pathogens carried by wild birds that are not covered in this book. Discuss your situation with your veterinarian for advice on prevention and treatments.

Bacterial Infections

Bacteria are part of life. Many are harmful, even lethal, but others perform necessary functions in your conure's body, including nutrient extraction and vitamin synthesis. It's when the bad ones run amok that illness occurs.

Bacteria are usually divided into two types: gram-negative and gram-positive. To oversimplify, gram-positive bacteria are typically harmless and normal for your bird, but gram-negative can cause illness. There are exceptions, but most of the usual bacterial infections in pet birds are caused by various gram-negative species.

Enterobacter

The most common are *Enterobacteriaceae,* which include the notorious *Escherichia coli.* *E. coli* exists in several different strains. Some are commonly found in the digestive tract of humans and other mammals, but *E. coli* does not belong in the digestive tract of parrots, and can cause severe illness, organ damage, and death if untreated. Symptoms of *E. coli* infection include lethargy, loss of appetite, and diarrhea. Affected birds need to be treated as soon

as possible with appropriate antibiotics or they will probably not survive.

Salmonella spp. are another common but potentially lethal group of enterobacter bacteria that can sicken your conure. Symptoms of *Salmonella* can be similar to that of *E. coli,* but severe or chronic infections might also manifest as central nervous system problems, arthritis, or joint pain. *Salmonella* is especially tricky, because it can exist in a sub-clinical carrier state in birds that appear completely healthy. The infection can then be passed to other birds or even humans. If you suspect *Salmonella,* test and treat your bird exactly as recommended by your veterinarian to clear up any sub-clinical infections.

Chlamydia

Chlamydia psittaci is a type of bacterium that causes severe or chronic disease in many species of birds, especially parrots. The disease it causes is known as chlamydiosis, psittacosis, or "parrot fever." When the infection affects birds other than parrots, it is called ornithosis. Despite the different names, they are all the same disease from the same bacterium. Chlamydiosis is a zoonotic disease, which means that it can be transmitted to humans, especially the elderly or immuno-suppressed. In humans, it causes mild to moderate flu-like symptoms, but usually responds quickly to antibiotics.

In birds, however, the infection can be sub-clinical in carrier birds, or can cause severe disease and death in susceptible individuals. Symptoms include lethargy, depression, dehydration, weight loss, green or yellow urates, difficulty breathing, and sinusitis. If left untreated, the bird will die. Antibiotic therapy can be effective, but the treatment must be monitored by a veterinarian, and must continue for at least forty-five days.

Fungal Infections

There are many types of disease-causing fungi, but two are most commonly implicated in illness in conures: *Candida albicans* and *Aspergillus* spp.

Candida is most common in hand-rearing chicks, but can sometimes affect adults. It is usually caused by a suppression of the immune system, most often when antibiotic therapy wipes out the healthy bacteria that are normal in a bird's crop. That is why veterinarians often prescribe antifungals along with antibiotics. Symptoms include a thickened crop, weight loss, and vomiting. Sometimes a cottage cheese-like plaque is visible in the bird's mouth. Prescription antifungals along with supplementary probiotics usually clear it up quickly.

Aspergillus spp. can cause a much more serious disease known as aspergillosis. *Aspergillus* fungi are found throughout the environment, and usually don't cause much trouble unless a bird is stressed, malnourished, or it has a compromised immune system. Moldy or musty seed and bedding are common sources of the fungi. Sometimes it strikes an otherwise healthy bird for no apparent reason, but usually there is some underlying challenge to the bird's immune system. Symptoms of the disease include respiratory difficulties, weight loss, and sometimes diarrhea. The bird might shake its head or stretch its neck and gape as if it is choking. Often, the first sign in a vocal parrot is loss of voice. It is a very difficult disease to treat. Lengthy treatments that include nebulizing the birds with drugs such as amphotericin B are sometimes successful, but require a sizeable commitment of time and money. Like many other diseases, prevention of infections is usually much easier than treatment.

Viral Infections

If your conure is healthy when you purchase it, and it's not exposed to other birds, then viral infections shouldn't pose much of a problem. There are a few viruses that can remain latent in conures, however, so awareness is crucial if your pet starts to exhibit signs of illness.

Oddly, the worst parrot viruses all begin with the letter "P," and are sometimes referred to as the "four P's." There are some testing protocols in use, but false negative results are possible, especially in birds not currently shedding the viral particles. Always discuss possible diagnostics with your veterinarian.

✔ Polyomavirus causes usually lethal infections in chicks, and typically less severe disease in adults. Symptoms that may appear include depression, loss of appetite, subcutaneous hemorrhages (bleeding under the skin), vomiting, and delayed crop emptying. Infected chicks usually die within 24 to 48 hours after exhibiting symptoms. Any that do survive may become carriers of the disease and spread the virus to others. Adult birds rarely become seriously ill or show signs of the disease, although they can be infected and become carriers. Adult birds may be able to clear the virus from their systems, but re-infection is possible. A vaccine is available for susceptible individuals.

✔ PBFD, or psittacine beak and feather disease, is a highly contagious and fatal DNA circovirus that can affect almost any species of parrot, although it is much less common in New World species such as conures. There are two forms of PBFD, chronic and acute. The acute form, which is most common in nestlings, often begins with depression, crop stasis, and deformities in emerging feathers, and usually results in death within a few days to a few weeks. In the chronic

form, which is more common in adult birds, there is a symmetric and progressive emergence of stunted or clubbed feathers. The beak can also be affected by abnormal growth, malformations, and areas of necrosis. The chronic form is also fatal, although some individuals can live for many years after the disease appears. There have been a few reported cases of New World parrots (mostly macaws and pionus) that have appeared to recover completely from PBFD.

✔ Pacheco's disease virus (PDV) is caused by an avian herpesvirus, and usually causes severe or fatal liver disease. There are several strains of PDV—some strains kill over 80 percent of exposed parrots, yet others will cause just a few deaths and scattered illness. Symptoms include sudden death, depression, diarrhea (which might contain blood), green or yellow urates, and tremors or seizures. Unfortunately, conures, especially Patagonians and Nandays, can be asymptomatic carriers of the disease, and can shed the virus intermittently and cause future outbreaks. There are vaccines available, which appear to prevent illness, but not necessarily infection. What this means is that a vaccinated parrot won't become sick itself if exposed to the disease, but it might be able to pass the disease on to other birds.

✔ Proventricular Dilatation Disease, or PDD, is a fatal disease of parrots that until recently had no known cause. In the summer of 2008, researchers at the University of California, San Francisco, used DNA sequencing techniques to isolate a new bornavirus, which they have named Avian Bornavirus (ABV). This virus, which is in the same family of viruses that causes encephalitis in cattle and horses, damages the nerves in the bird's gastrointestinal tract. It destroys the ventriculus and proventriculus (the muscular stomachs), causing the bird to slowly starve to death, no matter how much food it consumes. Symptoms include progressive weight loss, vomiting, passing undigested food in the droppings, and crop impactions. In some cases, brain and heart damage occur, causing neurological symptoms such as weakness, lameness, and seizures. An infected bird can show any combination of these symptoms. There's currently no cure, but the UCSF researchers have also developed a diagnostic test to isolate infected individuals. Some research has shown success in reversing acute symptoms through the use of special diets and human COX-2 inhibiting drugs to reduce inflammation in the gastric tract, leading to the hope that PDD will become a survivable disease.

✔ Conure Bleeding Syndrome is, as the name implies, unique to conures. It appears to be endemic in several species, including the Blue-crowned, Peach-fronted, Orange-fronted, and Patagonian conures. Researchers believe it is tied to a virus, probably a type of retrovirus, but that theory has not yet been proven. It does appear that calcium deficiencies can trigger the onset in susceptible individuals, so careful dietary controls are important. The disease is characterized by immature or improperly formed blood cells that cause internal hemorrhaging, eventually leading to death. External symptoms include extreme weakness, shortness of breath, diarrhea, lack of coordination, and bleeding from the nose or mouth. Because many viruses are difficult to detect and prevent, it's important to protect your conure from exposure to strange birds or circumstances that could pose a risk. Always quarantine new birds, and wash your hands thoroughly before handling your pet.

If your conure is injured or ill, there are some critical steps you can take to help it through the crisis. The single most important thing that a sick or hurt bird requires is heat. If you can help keep it warm, it can turn all its resources to survival.

The best way to keep your bird warm and calm is to place it on a towel inside its travel carrier, and then place the carrier on top of a heating pad. First lay the heating pad on a counter or heat resistant surface, and set the heat to low. Place the carrier on top of the heating pad so that the pad covers only about half of the carrier bottom. This will allow your pet to move off the heat to the cooler side if it becomes overheated. Drape a towel across the top to hold in heat and humidity, and to allow the bird to rest without distractions.

Keep the temperature between 85 and 90°F (30–32°C). If necessary, turn the heating pad to medium setting. If it's too warm, pull the towel back a bit to allow more heat to escape, and reduce heat to low setting.

Once your conure is settled into the warm carrier, contact your veterinarian (or an after-hours emergency service—don't wait until morning!) and describe the injury or the symptoms. More than likely, you'll need to bring the bird into the clinic. If it's cool outside, don't forget to heat up your car first, and fasten the carrier securely with a seat belt so sudden stops don't cause it to tip over.

The veterinarian will need a clear understanding of just what's wrong. Some things, like a broken bone or bleeding wound, will be quite obvious. In the case of poisoning or sudden illness, be prepared to answer the following questions.

✔ How old is the bird?

✔ What is its usual diet, and when did it last eat?

✔ Has it eaten or chewed on anything different lately?

✔ How long have the symptoms been present?

✔ Was anyone in the household using any fume or odor producing chemicals or devices?

✔ Are any people or animals in the household also ill?

✔ Did the conure have any direct contact with other animals, either in the home or outdoors?

These and other questions will help the doctor zero in on possible causes, and order any appropriate diagnostics. Do not ever attempt to treat a sick bird with over-the-counter antibiotics, dog or cat drugs, or any leftover human medications. At best, you run the risk of further weakening the bird or masking important symptoms. At worst, you

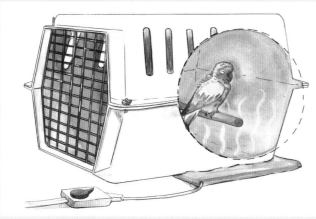

A makeshift hospital cage can supply heat until you can transport the bird to a veterinarian.

FIRST AID

might kill your pet with your attempts to play veterinarian.

But what about emergency first aid? There are some things you can do before heading out the door to the clinic.

✔ Bleeding: First, assess the cause and severity of the injury if possible. Minor bleeding from a chipped beak or broken blood feather might resolve on its own without intervention. If it's just a few very tiny drops of blood, calm the bird and observe for a few minutes to see if it stops on its own. Remember that a stressed or strug-gling bird will bleed faster due to its higher heart rate. If it doesn't stop, a dab of styptic powder or cornstarch can help coagulate bleeding from beaks or toenails, but don't use these on skin wounds. For larger wounds, rinse away debris with hydrogen peroxide if necessary, and hold gentle pressure with a gauze pad or clean towel until you can transport to the vet for further treatment. Broken blood feathers that don't stop bleeding need to be pulled. Use a pair of needle-nosed pliers or locking forceps, and pull the bro-ken feather in the direction of growth.

✔ Burns: For small and minor burns, rinse the area carefully in cool water, and apply a water-based topical antibiotic burn cream if recom-mended by your veterinarian. Do not use oil-based formulas, as these will permanently damage feathers. If the burned area is large, or if there's any sign of blistering or severe damage, transport the conure to a veterinarian for further treatment including fluid and antibiotic therapy as needed.

✔ Broken bones: Never attempt to splint a broken bone on your own. Immobilize the area if possible by tucking the bird between soft rolled towels, and transport to a veterinarian immediately.

Broken wings can be gently immobilized with roll gauze, but this is only a temporary measure until a veterinarian can splint the wing.

✔ Shock: Place the bird into a heated carrier as mentioned above. If the shock is due to trauma, such as flying into a wall or being attacked by another animal, your pet will need further treat-ment, possibly radiographs, steroid therapy, or antibiotics.

✔ Heat exhaustion: Prevent this by using com-mon sense, and never leave your pet unattended in a locked car, even if the windows are rolled down. If your conure is ever exposed to high heat, and shows symptoms such as panting, trembling, holding its wings away from its body, or loss of coordination, it's imperative to bring down the dangerously high body temperature. Stand the bird gently into a shallow dish of cool (not cold) water and call your veterinarian. Birds dissipate heat through their feet and legs, so the cool water can help, but don't leave it unat-tended—the parrot could have a seizure or loss of balance and drown, even in a shallow crock.

SELECT CONURE SPECIES AND DESCRIPTIONS

Taxonomy is the science of classifying things into a hierarchal order.

Taxonomy comes from the Greek *taxis* (order) + *nomos* (science). An easy way to think of it is as a giant filing system that allows scientists to keep everything in a logical place for retrieval and study. But it's not just scientists who benefit from this system. Taxonomy allows us to speak a universal language of sorts when we discuss different species, rather than relying upon easily misunderstood common names.

For example, let's say you wish to purchase a Half-moon conure. You browse the classifieds, but the only conure for sale is an Orange-fronted. If you and the seller were speaking the same language, you'd know that you're both using different names for the same bird, *Aratinga canicularis.* That's why breeders often use the scientific names—not to impress folks with their grasp of Latin, but to head off any confusion regarding the bird in question.

Understanding Taxonomy

As mentioned in the Introduction to this book, all but a few conures fall into the genera *Aratinga* and *Pyrrhura*. Patrick G. Coyle Jr., in his book *Understanding the Life of Birds*, uses a wonderful analogy to explain taxonomical classifications. All conures are, of course, birds, which fall under the Class Aves. Class could be compared to the county you live in. Next comes Order, which would compare to a city name. Conures belong to the Order Psittaciformes, which includes all parrots. After Order is Family, or street name in this analogy. Conures are in the Psittacidae Family. Some Families are broken into smaller sub-types known as Subfamilies, similar to adding a "North" or "South" designation to your street name. Conures are in the Subfamily Psittacinae.

Blue-crowned conure.

Okay, we're almost at your door! After Sub-family comes Genus, analogous to a house number. That's where *Aratinga* and *Pyrrhura* fit into the picture. After Genus is Species, which equates to an apartment number.

Finally, the smallest division left is Sub-species, which would be a room in the apartment. Can you see how neatly the system allows you to zero in on a specific bird, without confusion or vagueness?

Now that the system makes some sense to you, let's take a look at some common pet species mentioned in the Introduction.

Genus *Aratinga*

Blue-Crowned (or Sharp-Tailed) Conure

Scientific Name: *Aratinga a. acuticaudata*
Range: Northern Venezuela south to Paraguay, Uruguay, and northern Argentina.
Size: About 14 inches (36 cm) long.
Description: Mostly green with dull blue head; sometimes the breast is tinged with blue as well. Horn colored upper mandible, blackish lower mandible. These birds are extremely intelligent, easy to tame, and make affectionate pets.

Brown-Throated (or St. Thomas) Conure

Scientific Name: *Aratinga p. pertinax*
Range: North from Panama down through northern South America into parts of Venezuela. Endemic to the island of Curacao, and introduced to other islands including Aruba and St. Thomas.
Size: About 10 inches (25 cm) in length.
Description: Green with yellow-orange on the forehead, face, and chin. Orange tinged abdomen, and crown sometimes tinged with blue. Beaks are horn colored to gray. Once rare in aviculture, it's being bred with more frequency in recent years.

Brown-throated conure.

Cactus conure.

Cactus Conure

Scientific Name: *Aratinga c. cactorum*
Range: Mostly north-eastern Brazil.
Size: About 10 inches (25 cm) in length.
Description: An attractive bird that slightly resembles a Senegal parrot in coloring. Mostly green overparts with bright orange abdomen. Upper breast and head are a soft brown. Crown sometimes suffused with blue. Beak is horn-colored to light gray. Uncommon but available in aviculture.

Cherry-Headed (or Red-Masked) Conure

Scientific Name: *Aratinga erythrogenys*
Range: South-western Ecuador and northern Peru.

Cherry-headed conure.

Size: About 13 inches (33 cm) in length.

Description: Mostly green except for striking red on its head, shoulders, under-wing coverts, and thighs. Adult birds have more extensive red than juveniles. Beak is horn-colored. Uncommon but available.

Dusky-Headed Conure

Scientific Name: *Aratinga weddellii*

Range: Wide range throughout the Amazon basin, including Ecuador, Peru, Bolivia, and western Brazil.

Size: about 11 inches (28 cm) in length.

Description: Plumage is mostly green with a grayish-blue head and yellowish diffusion on the abdomen. Irises are pale gray, and a broad area

Finsch's conure.

of white skin surrounds the eye. Beak is black. Known as one of the quieter large conures.

Finsch's Conure

Scientific Name: *Aratinga finschi*

Range: Southern Nicaragua to western Panama.

Size: About 11 inches (28 cm) in length.

Description: Mostly green with red forehead and crown. Red band across throat and at bend of wing. Immature birds have much less red. Beak is horn-colored.

Dusky-headed conure.

Golden-capped conure.

Jenday conure.

Golden–Capped Conure

Scientific Name: *Aratinga a. auricapilla*
Range: eastern Brazil
Size: about 12 inches (30 cm) in length.
Description: Primarily green, with a reddish facemask that fades to yellow on the crown. Abdomen is suffused with deep orange-red feathers. Beak is gray-black. These are common birds in American aviculture, but are rare and endangered in their native range. Captive breeding and reintroduction programs might be their only hope of survival if free ranging populations continue to decline. Relatively quiet compared to some *Aratingas*.

Jenday Conure

Scientific Name: *Aratinga jandaya*
Range: North-eastern Brazil
Size: About 12 inches (30 cm) in length.
Description: Mostly green back and upper wings, with head, neck, and upper breast deep yellow to yellow-orange, deepening to red-orange on lower abdomen and lower back. A striking beautiful and commonly bred bird with wonderful pet potential. Some ornithologists have postulated that the Golden-capped, Jenday, and Sun conures are actually conspecific, meaning they are all subspecies of one single species. To date, they are still considered

Mitred conure.

Orange-Fronted (or Half-Moon) Conure

Scientific Name: *Aratinga c. canicularis*
Range: Western Central America from Mexico south to Costa Rica.
Size: About 9½ inches (24 cm) in length.
Description: Mostly green bird with greenish-yellow breast and abdomen. Forehead is orange with blue band on crown. Beak is horn-colored with some black on lower mandible.

entirely separate species, but as I've said before, taxonomy can and does evolve and reclassify on a frequent basis as our knowledge grows.

Mitred Conure

Scientific Name: *Aratinga m. mitrata*
Range: Central and southern Peru down through central Bolivia and western Argentina.
Size: About 15 inches (38 cm) in length.
Description: A large conure that is mostly green with heavy red feathering on its head, sometimes extending throughout its chest. Immatures are all green. Beak is horn-colored. They can be quite noisy, but are known as sweet and affectionate pets.

Orange-fronted conure.

Peach-fronted conure.

Red-fronted conure.

Peach-Fronted Conure

Scientific Name: *Aratinga a. aurea*

Range: Widespread throughout Brazil, ranging as far south as eastern Bolivia and northern Paraguay.

Size: about 10 inches (25 cm) in length.

Description: Coloring is very similar to the Orange-fronted, although this species is slightly larger and has an entirely black beak. They are common in the pet trade, and are reputed to be on the quieter side of the conure noise spectrum.

Red-Fronted Conure

Scientific Name: *Aratinga w. wagleri*

Range: Widely distributed along the western coast of South America, from Venezuela down through southern Peru.

Size: About 14 inches (36 cm) in length.

Description: Similar in appearance to the Mitred, but this species has less red on the head and body. It is also slightly smaller than the Mitred. Juvenile birds show little red until adult molt. Not common in aviculture.

Sun Conures

Scientific Name: *Aratinga solstitialis*

Range: From the Guianas through north-western Brazil.

Size: About 12 inches (30 cm) in length.

Description: One of the most colorful conures, the Sun is primarily a striking mix of bright yellow and deep orange, with dark blue wing primaries and intermittent green in the wings and tail. Beak is black. Immature birds can be mostly green, with full coloration not appearing until the bird matures. These conures are highly prized as pets; although noisy, they're affectionate and intelligent.

White-eyed conure.

White-Eyed Conure

Scientific Name: *Aratinga l. leucophthalma*

Range: Widely distributed over northern South America from the Guianas south through northern Argentina and Paraguay.

Size: About 13 inches (33 cm) in length.

Description: Mostly green with widely scattered red feathers on the head, neck, and carpal wing bend. Beak is horn-colored with slight blackish-gray at tips of mandibles. They are known to be affectionate and gentle, but noisy.

Sun conure.

Genus *Pyrrhura*

Black-Capped Conure

Scientific Name: *Pyrrhura r. rupicola*
Range: Central and south-eastern Brazil and northern Bolivia.
Size: about 10 inches (25 cm) in length.
Description: Mostly dark green, with a broad band of white-scalloped dark feathers around the neck and lower breast, giving the appearance of a bib. The head is a greenish-brown,

Green-cheeked conure.

Black-capped conure.

more olive on the sides. Carpal wing bend and primary coverts are red. Beak is gray.

Green-Cheeked Conure

Scientific Name: *Pyrrhura m. molinae*
Range: Brazil and parts of Bolivia and Argentina.
Size: About 10 inches (25 cm) in length.
Description: Mostly dark green, with a wide bib of green-black feathers scalloped with ivory reaching down to a dark green lower abdomen

Maroon-bellied conure.

sometimes flecked with maroon. Head and nape are brown, cheeks bright green. Small bird with a lot of confidence and personality, common in the pet trade.

Maroon-Bellied Conure

Scientific Name: *Pyrrhura f. frontalis*

Range: South-eastern Brazil, Uruguay, north-eastern Argentina, and eastern Paraguay.

Size: About 10 inches (25 cm) in length.

Description: Similar to the Green-cheeked, but the scalloped feathers have a pale yellow and bronze cast. Ear coverts are tan, and most individuals have patches of maroon on the lower abdomen. Head is mostly dark green. Uncommon but available in the pet trade.

Maroon-Tailed (or Black-Tailed or Souance's) Conure

Scientific Name: *Pyrrhura m. melanura*

Range: Widely distributed through Colombia, southern Venezuela, northern Brazil, Ecuador, and north-eastern Peru.

Size: about 10 inches (25 cm) in length.

Description: Mostly dark green, with a scalloped band of white-tipped dark brownish-green feathers around the neck. Forehead and crown dark brown mottled with green. Upper tail black with dark green at base. Underside of tail is maroon. Primary wing coverts are red. Beak is grayish brown. Once very uncommon in aviculture, now more readily available due to successful captive breeding.

Maroon-tailed conure.

Painted conure.

Painted Conure

Scientific Name: *Pyrrhura picta*

Range: Guianas to Venezuela, south to southern Peru, and northern Bolivia. Also some parts of Colombia.

Size: About 8½ inches (21.5 cm) in length.

Description: This is the smallest of the conure group, weighing about 55 grams (1.8 oz.), approximately the same weight as a large English budgie. It is also one of the most attractive of the *Pyrrhura* genus. Mostly dark green on the back, its lower abdomen is more olive green, suffused with maroon. The characteristic scalloped bib feathers of the *Pyrrhura* are present, but in this bird they're sharply defined and triangular in appearance. The forehead is dark blue, changing to dark brown with scattered blue infusions on the crown. Sides of the face are deep maroon, with dark periorbital rings, black beak, and buff colored ear coverts. Bend of the wing is bright red. Although relatively common in the wild, this species was almost unheard of in aviculture until recent years, when captive breeding began to have some successes. Still rare, but occasionally available.

Other Genera

Queen of Bavaria's (or Golden) Conure

Scientific Name: *Guaruba guarouba* (some older sources list as *Aratinga guarouba*)

Range: North-eastern Brazil

Size: About 14 inches (36 cm) in length.

Description: This is a heavy-bodied bird with a large head, massive beak, and blunted tail that give it an appearance more like a small macaw than a large conure. It is a bright golden yellow, except for green in its flight feathers. Beak is horn-colored. Immature birds might have scattered green feathers throughout. It is extremely intelligent, loving, and exceptionally playful. Unfortunately, as noted earlier, it is also extremely endangered and should be kept in species management programs, not pet homes. However, it is possible to obtain one as a pet, even though this is a choice I wouldn't recommend.

Nanday Conure

Scientific Name: *Nandayus nenday*

Range: South-eastern Bolivia, Brazil, Paraguay, and northern Argentina.

Size: About 12 inches (30 cm) in length.

Description: Mostly bright green, with black head and beak. Throat and upper breast blue, abdomen an olive green. Red thighs. Nandays are one of the most common conures, both in

Queen of Bavaria's conure.

Nanday conure.

Size: About 14 to 16 inches (36–40 cm) in length.

Description: These are the only species in the genera *Enicognathus.* They are similar in coloring to the Maroon-bellied conure *Pyrrhura f. frontalis,* but the *Enicognathus* have a cere covered in thick, short feathers. The Austral is smaller and slightly duller in color than the Slender-bill, but the most striking difference is in the beaks: Australs have a normal hook bill, but the Slender-billed (as its name suggests) has a long, narrow, and only slightly curved upper mandible. The nares and forehead and an area ringing the eyes is dark maroon in the Austral, more reddish in the Slender-bill. Both species

the wild and in captivity. They are prolific breeders and affectionate pets. Often considered one of the noisiest conures, but birds kept singly are sometimes quieter.

Austral Conure and Slender-Billed Conure

Scientific Name: *Enicognathus f. ferrugineus, Enicognathus leptorhynchus*

Range: Central to southern Chile (Slender-billed), southern Chile to Tierra del Fuego (Austral).

Slender-billed conure.

Patagonian conures.

are uncommon, but have a reputation as being gentle and sweet, and can be good talkers.

Patagonian Conure and Greater Patagonian Conure

Scientific Name: *Cyanoliseus p. patagonus, Cyanoliseus p. bloxami*

Range: Central Chile, northern Argentina, occasionally Uruguay.

Size: About 18 to 20 inches (46–51 cm) in length.

Description: This single species genus contains three recognized subspecies, very similar except for size and degree of coloration. The Patagonian and Andean Patagonian are similar in size, while the Greater Patagonian is larger. These birds are mostly a dark olive-brown, with yellow and red on the abdomen. In the Greater, a white band of feathers extends across the neck. The Lesser Patagonian has less extensive white markings, and the Andean has none. All subspecies have a feathered cere and large bare eye ring. Patagonians are very pleasant and attractive birds, but unfortunately one of the loudest of the conures. This is not a bird designed for apartment living.

Periodicals

Bird Talk/Birds USA
P.O. Box 6050
Mission Viejo, CA 92690
(949) 855-8822
www.animalnetwork.com

Bird Times
Pet Publishing, Inc.
4642 West Market Street, #368
Greensboro, NC 27407
(336) 292-4047
www.petpublishing.com/birdtimes

The AFA Watchbird
American Federation of Aviculture, Inc.
P.O. Box 91717
Austin, TX 78709-1717
(512) 585-9800
www.afabirds.org/watchbird.shtml

Organizations

Association of Avian Veterinarians
P.O. Box 811720
Boca Raton, FL 33481
(561) 393-8901
www.aav.org

American Federation of Aviculture
P.O. Box 91717
Austin, TX 78709-1717
(512) 585-9800
www.afabirds.org

International Conure Association
P.O. Box 70123
Las Vegas, NV 89170
www.conure.org/ica/

Helpful Web Sites

www.upatsix.com
www.birdsnways.com

Manufacturers and Suppliers

Cage Catchers
Div. of Handy Wacks Corp.
100 E Averill Street
Sparta, MI 9345
(800) 445-4434
www.cage-catchers.com
(custom-made cage bottom liners)

Pretty Bird International, Inc.
31010 Foxhill Avenue
P.O. Box 177
Stacy, MN 55079
(800) 356-5020
www.prettybird.com
(seed, formulated diets, and treats)

Kaytee Products, Inc.
521 Clay Street
Chilton, WI 53014
(800) 669-9580
www.kaytee.com
(seed, formulated diets, and treats)

L'Avian Pet Products
Highway 75 S
P.O. Box 359
Stephen, MN 56757
(800) 543-3308
(L'Choice bird diets)

Prevue Pet Products, Inc.
224 North Maplewood
Chicago, IL 60612
(800) 243-3624
(pet and breeding cages)

Rolf C. Hagen U.S.A. Corp
50 Hampden Road
Mansfield, MA 02048
(800) 225-2700
www.pubnix.net/~mhagen
(Various bird products, seed diets)

Roudybush
340 Hanson Way
Woodland, CA 95776
(800) 326-1726
www.roudybush.com
(pelleted diets)

Important Note
   Please remember that conures are intelligent and endangered birds. They require a substantial amount of care, and are not low maintenance pets. They should never be purchased on a whim. If you are ever unable to care for your conure, please contact a local bird shelter for guidance. Releasing a non-indigenous bird into the wild is against the law in most states, and it is unlikely a domestically raised conure could survive outdoors.

INDEX

Adult birds, 9
Air quality, 31
Antibiotics, 68, 70, 74–75
Aspergillosis, 70
Austral conure, 11, 89
Avian Bornavirus, 72
Avian veterinarians, 20

Bacterial infections, 68
Bird fairs, 15
Biting, 46, 55
Black-capped conure, 10, 85
Bleeding, 72, 75
Blue-crowned conure, 10, 72, 78
Body language, 55
Bolborhynchus parakeets, 6
Bones, broken, 75
Breathing difficulty, 16, 68, 70, 72
Breeders, 14
Brotogeris parakeets, 6
Brown-throated conure, 10, 78
Burns, 75

Cactus conure, 10, 79
Cages
  bar spacing, 24–25
  cleaning, 33
  covers, 30
  placement, 23, 26, 28
  sizing, 24
  substrates, 33
  travel, 30
  types, 23–24
Calcium deficiency, 31, 72
Carolina parakeet , 6
Cherry-headed conure, 10, 79–80
Chewing, destructive, 46
Chlamydiosis, 18, 68
Choosing a healthy bird, 13
Cleaning supplies, 33
Command, off, 49
Command, step up, 49–50, 55
Conurus , 5–6

Diarrhea, 17, 68, 70, 72
Diets
  cooking, 64–65

formulated (pelleted), 60
fruits and vegetables, 61–62
grains and beans, 61
people foods, 62–63
seed, 57–58
Disinfection, 34
Droppings, 16–17, 68, 72
Dusky-headed conure, 10, 80

Emergency kit, 30–31
Escherichia coli, 68
Extinct species, 6–7

Feather damage, 16, 70, 72
Finsch's conure, 10, 80
First aid, 74–75
Free flight, 48–49
Fumes, 27
Fungal infections, 70

Golden-capped conure, 10, 81
Golden conure (*see* Queen of Bavaria's conure)
Green-cheeked conure, 10, 85

Half-moon conure (*see* Orange-fronted conure)
Health guarantees, 19
Heat exhaustion, 75
Height dominance, 49
Household hazards, 27, 48
Hybrid conures, 11
Hypocalcemia, 58

Importation, 7
International Conure Association, 5–6
Internet, 19

Jenday conure, 10, 81

Labeling, 50
Ladder game, 50
Lethargy, 16, 67, 68
Life expectancy, 57
Lighting, 31
Louisiana parakeet, 6

Maroon-bellied conure, 10, 86
Maroon-tailed conure, 10, 86
Mitred conure, 10, 82

Nanday conure, 9, 11, 72, 88–89
Nutrients, functions, and sources, 59

Operant conditioning, 50
Orange-fronted conure, 10, 72, 77, 82

Painted conure, 6, 10, 87
Parasites, 68
Parrot behavioralist, 55
Patagonian conure, 6, 9, 11, 72, 90
Peach-fronted conure, 10, 72, 83
Perches, 28–29
Personality, 8, 45–46
Pet stores, 14
Play, importance of, 37
Play, interactive games, 42–43
Playstands, 41–42
Poisonous plants, 27
Polyuria, 17
Protein, complete, 61
Psittacosis (*see* Chlamydiosis)

Quaker parakeet, 6
Quarantine, 18, 21
Queen of Bavaria's conure, 6, 10–11, 88

Recipes, 64–65
Red-fronted conure, 10, 83

Salmonella, 68
Screaming, 46, 53–55
Seizures, 72
Sharp-tailed conure (*see* Blue-crowned conure)
Shock, 75
Sick birds, 13, 15–18

Slender-billed conure, 11, 89–90
St. Thomas conure (*see* Brown-throated conure)
Sun conures, 10, 81, 84

Taxonomy, 5–6, 77–78
Teflon toxicity, 27
Temperature, 74–75
Thick-billed parrot, 6
Toxins, food, 61–62
Toys
  choosing, 37–40
  foot toys, 41
  making, 40
  simple, 40
Training
  bridge, 51
  cue, 51
  reward, 51
  speech, 50
  tricks, 50–53
Transporting birds, 19–20

Unweaned chicks, 9

Veterinary exam, 20, 53
Viruses
  Conure Bleeding Syndrome, 58–59, 72
  Pacheco's Disease, 72
  Polyoma, 70
  Proventricular Dilatation Disease, 72
  Psittacine Beak and Feather Disease, 70–72
Vitamin A deficiency, 58
Vocal ability, 8, 50

Water, 8, 63
Weight, 17, 20, 68, 70, 72
White-eyed conure, 10, 84
Wild Bird Conservation Act , 7
Wild parrots, 47
Wing clipping, 48

Zinc toxicity, 25–26, 29, 39
Zoonotic diseases, 68

About the Author

Gayle Soucek has been keeping and breeding a variety of exotic birds for over twenty years. She is the author of six books and numerous magazine articles on avian husbandry, nutrition, breeding, and disease, and is a contributing writer for *www.webvet.com*. Gayle is past-president of the Midwest Avian Research Expo, the Midwest Congress of Bird Clubs, and the Northern Illinois Parrot Society. She resides near Chicago with her husband, birds, dogs, and one very laid-back cat.

Cover Photos

Shutterstock: front cover, back cover, inside front cover, inside back cover.

Photo Credits

Connie Summers/Paulette Johnson: pages 2–3, 4, 12, 13, 15, 17, 18, 26, 32, 35, 36, 38, 42, 43, 44, 47, 48, 51, 52, 54, 55, 56, 58, 60, 63, 71, 73, 76, 84 (left), 91, 93; Shutterstock: page 66; Pieter van den Hooven: pages 5, 6, 7 (top left and bottom right), 8, 9, 11, 22, 23, 24, 29, 30, 34, 37, 41, 45, 57, 61, 62, 67, 69, 77, 78, 79 (top left and right and bottom), 80 (left and right), 81 (left and right), 82 (left and right), 83 (left and right), 84 (right), 85 (left and right), 86, 87 (left and right), 88, 89 (left and right), 90, 95.

All inquiries should be addressed to:
Barron's Educational Series, Inc.
250 Wireless Boulevard
Hauppauge, NY 11788
www.barronseduc.com

ISBN-13: 978-0-7641-4366-3
ISBN-10: 0-7641-4366-2

Library of Congress Catalog Card No. 2009013889

Library of Congress Cataloging-in-Publication Data
Soucek, Gayle.
   Conures : a complete pet owner's manual / Gayle Soucek.
       p. cm.
   Includes bibliographical references and index.
   ISBN-13: 978-0-7641-4366-3
   ISBN-10: 0-7641-4366-2
   1. Conures. I. Title.

   SF473.C65S68 2009
   636.6'865–dc22   2009013889

Printed in China
9 8 7 6 5 4 3 2 1